Counterfeiter

Counterfeiter

THE STORY OF A ~*Master*~ FORGER

Charles Black
Michael Horsnell

St. Martin's Press
New York

Library of Congress Cataloging-in-Publication Data

Black, Charles.
     Counterfeiter / Charles Black with Michael Horsnell.
        p.   cm.
     ISBN 0-312-03805-4
      1. Black, Charles, 1928– . 2. Counterfeits and counterfeiting.
  I. Horsnell, Michael. II. Title.
HG335.B55   1990
364.1'33—dc20
[B]   89-24115
                                        CIP

First published in Great Britain by New English Library.

First U.S. Edition
10 9 8 7 6 5 4 3 2 1

Preface

In Scotland Yard's celebrated Black Museum of criminal artefacts, where over 500 items are preserved at a constant temperature of sixty-two degrees, a special place is reserved for a set of printing plates, a remarkable series of forged bank-notes, and a cunningly hollowed out kitchen door once used to conceal some of them. They lack the gruesome drama of relics such as the bath in which mass murderer Dennis Nilsen disposed of some of his victims, the revolver with which Ruth Ellis shot her lover, the Western Union telegram announcing Dr. Crippen's arrest at sea, and the ropes which hanged a collection of nineteenth-century murderers. But they testify to a far more dangerous threat to the health of a nation than murder. Currency counterfeiting can sap its confidence by undermining its economy, as Hitler realised when he ordered the production of the famous "white fivers" with which he planned to flood Britain during World War II.

The comparatively undramatic counterfeiting artefacts in question, devotedly preserved in the windowless museum by its curator Bill Waddell, are part of the Forgeries and Counterfeits display maintained for posterity and the edification of detectives at Scotland Yard. Some items are amusing, such as the set of Belgian francs on which the forger made the mistake of spelling franc with the eleventh letter of the alphabet. Others are plain amateur, like the postal order altered from 3/6d to 8/6d which the forger tried to cash at a post office. But the plates and notes with which this book is concerned are in a different category. They were once the property of Charles Black, a master counterfeiter

5

who devised and developed a method of photo-lithography to forge currency of unparalleled quality. Their excellence literally drew whistles of approbation from the police officers and Treasury officials who examined them.

The twenty-dollar United States bills preserved at the museum, each bearing different serial numbers, are samples from an 85,000 dollar cache found in the false bottom of a box of potatoes, together with printing plates and negatives concealed in the hollowed out bottom of the kitchen door at Black's home in Garden Road, Bromley, Kent. They have each been overstamped "Forgery" by the police to obviate any risk of accidental reissue. Underneath the kitchen door, on display, has been placed a mirror to help detectives appreciate the finer points of criminal concealment. Another 3.5 million dollars were found in a concealed section of a brick garage at a house in Pagham, Sussex, where Black printed the notes with an accomplice. This vast amount of counterfeit currency was waiting to be distributed to criminal contacts throughout the world and more was to be printed at the rate of 2 million dollars per month. At the time of his arrest Black, who was charging fourteen per cent of the face value of his product, was well on course to the making of a fortune.

Overcoming such security devices as the watermark and metal strip in sterling and the "invisible" blue and red background flecks in the filigree-bedecked American dollar, he demonstrated better than any of his predecessors that anything created by the hand of one man may be imitated by the hand of another. That is the dilemma which has confronted bank-note designers since the Bank of England conducted its search with the assistance of the Royal Society of Arts in 1797 for the "inimitable note".

Not until 1836 did the offences of coining and forgery cease to carry the death penalty; indeed in 1820 the ultimate sentence was carried out on forty-six people for forging or, mainly, for the passing of counterfeit notes – some of which were discovered, unhappily too late, to be authentic. Black,

6

who possessed what one arresting officer described as the "counterfeiting skills of an angel", received ten years at the Old Bailey. At his trial a United States Treasury expert said he regarded the forgeries as the best ever produced – so good in fact that they rendered obsolete a new multi-million-dollar machine then under development to detect counterfeit currency.

Fifteen storeys above the Black Museum at Scotland Yard are the offices of the counterfeit currency squad, the only such specialist squad of its kind among the constabularies of England and Wales. More properly it is known as the National Central Office for the Suppression of Counterfeit Currency – and rather less reverently as the "funny money squad". The NCOSCC was born out of the Geneva Convention whose signatories agreed to form national centres, not only to investigate offences but also to establish data intelligence bases and liaise with the currency manufacturers. The elite squad, which has an enviable clear-up record, has overall responsibility for policing all currency offences in Britain – where a third of the world's bank-notes are printed – yet it is small enough to fit comfortably into an average-sized elevator. Only ten officers, under the direction of Detective Superintendent Keith Fletcher, are permanently attached.

Since modern police records began only 164 different, identifiable series of forged notes have been let loose upon the banking system and recovered by the banks themselves or the police. Of these only about one quarter have been of sufficiently high quality to merit the most serious attention. This means that at any one time there have rarely been more than two or three forgers at work. Only in the most recent years has Charles Black ceased to find himself automatically in the frame when the funny money squad turned up something special. The big south Londoner, born on Christmas Eve 1928, has retired from a remarkable career in which he launched two major counterfeiting operations.

Long before his emergence, the imitation of a bank-note was a laborious business requiring an engraver's expertise. Black's method of photo-lithography was something of a watershed in the art – taking it out of an era in which forgers wore green eyeshades and hung their dripping notes, according to legend, from a washing-line in the kitchen. In place of the engraver's tools, Black employed the camera in an ingenious way to make the negatives from which he printed his "funny money".

The introduction of new technology which he pioneered led to dramatic increases in the output of forged currency by the mid-eighties. In 1985 forgeries with a face value of 4.5 million pounds were seized by the police. But thanks to splendid detective work leading to successful prosecutions, that has dropped to its present level of 1.5 million pounds per year. More advanced technology, notably involving equipment such as the laser scanner, has threatened a new boom but, so far, those who have tried it have produced bank-notes which look pretty but feel bad. The notes have a flat feel because they are not embossed and are as convincing as a photographic reproduction is of an oil painting. By comparison Charles Black made an art of selecting the right paper, which fluoresced or not, according to the currency he was producing; and he developed methods of giving it the right texture with glycerine treatment, and a specially embossed surface which followed the contours of the ink – or at least appeared to.

The number of arrests for all offences relating to counterfeit currency in the United Kingdom – but over-whelmingly for the passing of it – is running at about 400 per year. The extraordinary vigilance by the police, which this figure denotes, has undoubtedly discouraged forgers in Britain. In fact only an estimated one per cent of the world's "funny" money is now believed to be printed in Britain whereas the United States wrestles with about eighty per cent of it. About sixty per cent in circulation is within the London area. How much room does it take up? All the

1.5 million pounds annually recovered in the UK, of which eighty per cent is from police raids on forgers' and distributors' premises and the rest through detection in the banking system, would fit into one and a half large suitcases if it were in twenty-pound notes.

Police expertise is not the only factor in making the job difficult for the counterfeiter. Like the hump on the back of the camel, the forger is stuck with his den wherever he chooses to base it. Thus he is perpetually vulnerable to detection. Charles Black's concealment techniques and caution enabled him to stay in production longer than many. But because of his reputation at Scotland Yard as a master of the art his career was effectively finished when he came out of prison and he was forced to go abroad in the mid-eighties in search of a safe haven.

Despite a constant revision of security measures, the US dollar will always remain the most popular note to imitate throughout the world. Sterling is less commonly found abroad though it is popular in Spain, particularly as payment for illicit drugs. Notes bearing the image of Her Majesty, though less impressive than those printed by Charles Black, often remain undetected in Spain because drug racketeers tend to scrutinise their money carelessly during a fast exchange of suitcases. Forged Dutch guilders are equally popular in the drugs market, notably of course in Amsterdam, and have been printed in Britain. In 1987, following a joint operation with the Dutch police, 610,000 Dutch notes of different denominations were seized in Britain and three people sent to prison.

With the boom in "plastic money" and indications of a cashless, credit card society emerging in the West, the counterfeiter has been forced to diversify in the late eighties. Thus the biggest police bust of a forger's den in 1988 uncovered not "funny money" but an astonishing array of forged documents. The den, in the East End of London, had been used to print birth certificates and passports, tailor-made for clients, with a bogus five-year travel history, together with marriage certificates and motoring documents. Criminals, ranging from terrorists to armed robbers, are prepared to pay highly for a new identity which can get them in and out of Britain, and illegal immigrants too are in the market for such documents.

Tax exemption certificates, television licence stamps, traveller's cheques and even shop trading stamps are also among the wares peddled by today's forger. Coins, too, have their place – often for use in vending machines – but only about 2,500 of these are annually recovered by the police. The diversity of counterfeiting in the late eighties does not, however, herald an end to the traditional forging of cash, not least because that is the currency of the criminal.

The Bank of England began its search for the foolproof note in response to the tide of forgeries which followed the issue of one- and two-pound notes in 1797 – about a century after the very first issue of British bank-notes. It was at the end of the eighteenth century, following restrictions on cash payments resulting from the Napoleonic War and a growing demand for gold, that low denomination notes were issued for the first time. This meant that the lower classes were handling bank-notes for the first time in their lives. Their inexperience and illiteracy provided an ideal climate for the forger and so the art of counterfeiting blossomed.

In the succeeding two centuries improvements in bank-note security and design have been introduced in order that the Bank of England may stay one step ahead of the forger and his constantly improving expertise in graphic arts technology. Traditional features such as watermarked paper, intaglio* printing and hand engraving have remained parts of the necessary security, but to these have been added such innovations as the contoured thread. By comparison the design of the earliest bank-notes was simple. Using the same basic design, bank-notes in 1745, for example, comprised £20 to £100 in steps of £10, plus £200, £300, £400, £500

* (a method of printing in which the image area is sunk into the surface of the plate)

10

and £1,000, and they were merely overprinted with different denominational features. Until 1957 the famous "white fiver", which had serious limitations as an anti-counterfeiting document, was printed on one side only. Whereas today the Queen, the Duke of Wellington, Florence Nightingale, William Shakespeare and Sir Christopher Wren have their parts to play in the design of notes ranging from five to fifty pounds, the only portrait to appear on British bank-notes until 1960 was that of Britannia who was adopted by the Bank of England as its seal in 1694. Not until 1928, with the issue of new ten shilling and one pound notes, did the Bank of England issue any currency printed on both back and front. The metallised thread was an innovation of World War II.

Today's notes, which emanate from a series started in 1970, have, of course, the most intricate of patterns which blend into pictures before reverting back to patterns. Different typefaces are used according to the denomination and carry watermarks of their particular historical figures. The thread has meanwhile become a complex feature.

But in its demanding search for new devices to produce the inimitable note, the Bank of England has been forced to remain within certain confines. The note must look like a note, it must be attractively designed, and it must be capable of high speed manufacture at its printing-works on the edge of Epping Forest at Loughton, Essex. Most importantly, however, it must be capable of manufacture within defined cost limits. With his own improving photo-lithographic expertise, these very limitations have permitted the forger to stay in the imitation game.

For most forgers, though, the disadvantages defeat all but the most skilful and determined. Even if he has the money, or the backing, to buy the necessary printing-machinery (or, indeed, the use of an otherwise bona fide printing-shop to work unauthorised midnight shifts), the counterfeiter is constantly faced with severe limitations. If his den remains undetected he still has the problem of disposing of his "funny money". He cannot, if he is astute, attempt to make a living out of passing it over shop-counters himself; nor must he casually enquire of a taxi-driver or a petrol-pump attendant if he would like to try a few samples. Instead he must rely on a small network of reliable distributors with their own criminal contacts, who will not grass if they are caught, to dispose of his output, which he must produce in bulk. Furthermore the forger must do nothing else of a criminal nature to invite the arrival of a police officer at his premises. All of these factors normally tend, sooner or later, to put the counterfeiter out of the imitation game.

Charles Black took on these overwhelming odds, flying by the seat of his pants at times to stay one step ahead of the police and a posse of treasury officials from across the world. What follows is his fascinating, instructive and often hilarious account of life as an unsurpassed master counterfeiter.

MICHAEL HORSNELL

1

By the time I drew the curtains round my cubicle at the end of a routine day in the print-shop at Her Majesty's Prison Leyhill, climbed onto my bunk and slipped on the earphones for the Radio Two late news bulletin, I was feeling as if I'd earned a mention in dispatches from the Civil Service. The job was relentlessly turning me into the scourge of the middle classes. Hot from the presses, which I rolled every day, were mountains of forms for the Department of Health and Social Security, explanatory notes for the Inland Revenue, and pamphlets for the Department of Employment – a litany of bumph eagerly awaited by battalions of Whitehall mandarins for the enlightenment of the fearful and bemused, sick, impoverished and unemployed. Life in the print-shop, as an involuntary guest of Her Majesty, was nothing if not worthy.

But I could scarcely afford to complain. Better the smell of ink, as a workmate, than the bouquet of carbolic in a landing-cleaner's bucket; better, too, a time-consuming job, of which I was the master, than spending twenty-three hours a day locked in my cell in one of the more fashionable penal institutions.

As prisons go, the open regime at Leyhill, a converted United States Air Force hospital in the Gloucestershire countryside at Wotton under Edge, offered a more comfortable kind of incarceration than most. With nearly eighteen months of my five-year sentence served, I could sense the oasis of parole on the horizon with as much relish as a poacher smelling the approach of dusk. Lost in the familiar daydreams of a prisoner counting the days, I scarcely heard the news from Washington of President Nixon's obstinate refusal to hand over the White House tapes to the Senate Watergate Committee. It was later in the bulletin, which was plugged into my ears, that I awoke with alarm from my reverie.

The newsreader announced that forged banknotes with an estimated face value of about ten million pounds, had been seized by police officers from the London-based regional crime squad in a raid on a house in Bromley, Kent.

I had good reason to take a deep breath as I imagined with consternation the intense police activity at the large modern residence in Garden Road – a fashionable back-water, situated within a tee-shot of Sundridge Park Golf Course. It happened to be my home.

The last time I had seen it was in February 1972 when I left to begin this, my second stretch in prison, for putting my signature to some stolen banker's drafts. With my throat beginning to run as dry as an empty well I imagined my wife Joan and our three children watching in disbelief as waves of policemen combed the property which I had bought as a vacant building plot for £2,000 in 1959. As police pushed aside the waist-high nettles in the three-quarters of an acre back garden and entered the shed they could have been no less astonished at what they discovered inside than if they had found a colony of fairies. It was in that cedar workshop, during the six months or so before I was sent to prison, that I had painstakingly assembled the finest forger's den in the history of counterfeiting.

Two men were helping police with their inquiries, I remember hearing the newsreader announce, and I wondered how long it would be before detectives called at the prison to invite me to add my assistance. The initial blankness with which I heard the news gave way to a labyrinth of nervous activity and I felt the blood beating in my temples.

With the backing of a West End club owner, who sold

the currency at fourteen per cent of its face value, partly through Mafia connections in the United States, and a number of European countries, I had built the den from scratch and taught Stanley Le Baigue, a distant relative of my wife, a method of photo-lithography. The expertise which he gained during our few months together allowed him to carry on printing while I was inside. So fine was the quality of the notes I designed that they drew whistles of admiration from the police officers and Treasury officials who descended on twenty-eight Garden Road, my wife told me later, when she visited me at Leyhill.

I had unfortunately been forced to retire from this blossoming business, in my back garden, after a time-bomb blew up in my face. While assembling the den, partly in the shed and partly in a study at the front of the house, I had travelled to the South Coast where, with an accomplice, I had passed a number of stolen banker's drafts to unsuspecting jewellers. It was in connection with these misdemeanours, unrelated to my incipient counterfeiting activities, that three detectives from Bournemouth, accompanied by a Metropolitan police liaison-officer, called at Garden Road in September 1971. By that stage Stanley and I had printed a creditable, but modest, stock of forged United States dollars with a face value of 500,000. Now there's nothing a policeman enjoys more, when given the opportunity, than to exercise his curiosity ransacking a suspect's personal effects. The four men who rummaged through my house that day were no exception and after seven hours of their closest attention, the place looked as if it had been hit by a mob of marauding Vikings. Fortunately, however, their efficiency didn't match their enthusiasm. Somehow they contrived to miss not only the forged currency in the shed, but the shed itself, and the study which was tucked away down a corridor, past the downstairs lavatory, and in which resided a large part of my illicit equipment. I was nevertheless marched off to Bournemouth for further questioning by the intrepid officers, who were doubtlessly confident they had all the evidence they needed to convict me of the offences I had committed on their patch, but who remain blissfully ignorant to this day of the promotion other, more sensational, discoveries might have earned them.

I was incarcerated for five weeks on remand in Dorchester Prison where I gainfully employed myself contemplating how to make numbering boxes to improve the output at Garden Road. These are small printing machines containing a series of wheels with numbers embossed on them literally to number the notes. Previously, I had laboriously hand-numbered them. I was then released on bail for nearly three months, a brief respite which I put to good purpose by returning to my den where I printed another $500,000, taught Stanley a few more tricks of the trade, and executed most of the art work on the new five-pound note. To my delight I was also able to make a numbering box for the United States dollars.

Having assumed, while on remand, that I had got away with my counterfeiting activities, I realised that my house would be as safe as the Bank of England from the attentions of the police throughout my forthcoming term of imprisonment.

By the time I had been convicted of my unconnected offences, and begun my five-year term at Leyhill, I had been able to bequeath a flourishing business to Stanley. In the following eighteen months Garden Road became the "World Headquarters" of forgery, as a jubilant Detective Superintendent George Sinclair of the regional crime squad described it to the press the day police swooped – Monday, July 23, 1973.

Incredibly throughout this period my wife Joan remained, like the officers from Bournemouth, in blessed ignorance of the operation, disapprovingly believing, as I had told her, that Stanley was printing soft-core pornography. Every day this increasingly familiar relative, the husband of a cousin, would arrive with sandwiches and vacuum flask, opening

16

his own key, and, with another key, unlocking the study which I had told her never to enter. He would disappear behind the door, which he relocked, for hours, venturing out only to use the lavatory and to spend further hours in the shed.

Behind the drawn curtain of my cubicle at Leyhill I suppressed my sense of shock – not just at the raid itself, but at the estimated ten-million pound output of the den. For Joan had told me by letter that Stanley was claiming difficulty in paying even the eighty pounds per month mortgage on the property. You can't choose your relatives. Amid my sense of shock I discovered a growing urge to take Stanley by the neck.

Meanwhile, with a degree of unease, I contemplated the future of prisoner 384315. The risk of being charged in connection with the counterfeiting operation was slight, I decided. Had not four police-officers searched my house from top to bottom when they arrested me eighteen months earlier and found nothing? Although I had been at home on remand for three months prior to my conviction who would believe I could have assembled a forger's den in such a short time? But would the Home Office be prepared to allow a man with a ten million pound connection – albeit only a residential one – to remain in an open prison? Big money tends to pay for escapes and no one knew for sure how much counterfeit currency was in circulation or who held it. I did not relish the thought of being regarded as a security risk and being transferred to the considerably harsher environment of a closed prison. It was the longest night I had spent since I discovered puberty and, in the cool hours before dawn, I sweated profusely.

A man much respected as a model prisoner by officers and inmates alike, I enjoyed a relatively privileged and comfortable incarceration. In the prison print-shop, to which I had been assigned without volunteering, I had demonstrated unusual aptitude, though I say it myself, and trained other prisoners to operate both the Heidelberg

17

letterpress machine and the new offset litho with which we performed sterling service on behalf of the Civil Service. Indeed my work, the irony of which was to dawn on my fellow captives and prison staff only the following morning, was to win me the Koestler award for industry and a cheque for seven guineas.

Convinced of my certain removal to a closed prison, I gloomily contemplated the loss of other important freedoms. Once a week I was permitted to attend a two-year course in catering at Brunel College, Bristol which promised a City and Guilds Certificate. There was also the relaxation and pleasure of breeding tropical fish at Leyhill, a hobby to which I devoted most of my spare time.

The tropical fish club which I had started there was the result of a conversation one day with a prison-officer who had complained about the impotence of two Malawi cichlids which he had bought for breeding. I managed to refrain from remarking that a man born out of wedlock, such as he, ought to be able to encourage a pair of fish to get their act together and offered to do the job for him. In a previous existence I had designed and developed thermostatically-controlled fish tanks at my parents' home and gone on to run a pet shop, with my wife, in South London where I had an attached workshop. The upshot was that I took over the officer's pair of reluctant mates and managed to breed a whole school of fish. My success and the subsequent inauguration of the Leyhill tropical fish club led to my acquiring the governor's permission for regular outings under escort to Bristol where I sold a variety of specimens for between twenty and thirty pence each, the proceeds being used to make the club self-supporting and provide it with new tanks. Now the governor had come to Leyhill from Wakefield Prison where there was a thriving tropical fish club, so I quickly established myself as a feather in his cap, promoting his nick as a model of penal perfection on Open Day, with my fabulous array of brightly coloured fish, snakes and toads. Now what kind of a life is that, you might ask, for a master forger of my calibre? Not much. But it's a whole lot more satisfactory than staring through the bars of Pentonville or Wormwood Scrubs, and I didn't fancy losing it in the wake of the bust at Garden Road.

As the night of the raid wore on, and throughout the following day when the national newspapers splashed the news across their front pages, I developed a deep sense of foreboding which was not alleviated by the banter of my associates. Could I change a fiver? I was asked several times by amused inmates. What was the rate of exchange for this or that currency? Where was I planning to spend my holidays? One officer made a ten-pound bet with another screw that yours truly would soon be staring at a twenty-foot wall from the wrong side. Rather like a man who had forecast eight draws but forgotten to post his pools coupon, I fancied keeping myself to myself that day as a stream of television pictures publicised my house and front garden.

Back at Garden Road, apparently, the neighbours were agog behind their lace curtains as battalions of perspiring policemen continued to relieve number twenty-eight of the treasury of British and foreign currency, which they found packed in cardboard boxes piled high to the study ceiling. Lorries carried away an array of equipment weighing several tons which, by any standards, was fit to rival that of the Royal Mint. Worried Bank of England officials arrived in limousines to inspect the premises, FBI agents handling Treasury matters flew in from Washington, and Australian and French Treasury men packed their suitcases.

Behind the suburban façade of twenty-eight Garden Road, overlooked by shrubbery and tall trees, and surrounded by the immaculately groomed homes of stockbrokers and bank managers, policemen found the study as claustrophobic as a submarine. The window was sealed against the light with tightly-fitting hardboard, and behind that were Venetian blinds, as well as a heavily lined set

19

of curtains. A large stainless steel sink, with three compartments for washing and printing negatives, was lodged against one wall, together with plate-making equipment and a light box. Underneath was a unit, plumbed into the toilet next door, which took water from the mains, heated and recirculated it for washing the prints. Opposite the door, which was also light-proofed, was a vertical graphic arts camera with four 500 tungsten halogen lamps on it – equipment which, when operating, turned the room into an oven. An Italian Incaf camera, with Sneider lenses, was also crammed in with filter boxes for colour separation which I had built. In addition, there were a flip-top plate-maker and a drying-cabinet with further colour-separation equipment on top. Against another wall there was a densitometer for measuring the density of emulsion on a negative, necessary for colour separation. With plates, negatives and boxes of finished notes of several nationalities and denominations, astonished police officers found it scarcely possible for more than one at a time to enter the room.

In the shed, which I had planted on deep concrete footings, police discovered the print-shop, the plates for different dollar notes, and fifty-pound and twenty-pound traveller's cheques drawn on Barclays, Lloyds and National Westminster Banks, as well as the excreta of the whole operation – a mountain of wastepaper from currency already printed. An offset litho machine, an eighteen-inch electric guillotine, a hand letterpress printing-machine, numbering boxes and a supply of magnetic ink completed the equipment packed into the shed.

It had been, I'm sure you'll agree, an extraordinary Aladdin's cave for the police to have missed when they first arrived to interview me in 1971.

The haul of counterfeit currency was the biggest ever seized in Europe, and the house the biggest forgery production centre in the world. It was a den which police, who linked their investigations with the FBI and Interpol, had been desperate to locate for some months. Their efforts, of course, had not been assisted by the fact that I was in prison and therefore my home was not under suspicion. Indeed so elusive was my den, that a theory behind the wave of counterfeiting which had been worrying Treasury officials in several countries, was that it was installed in a pantechnicon and was therefore frustratingly mobile.

The hunt for the forgers began after counterfeit English fivers flooded a number of holiday centres. Then, a disturbing number were discovered in Central London where they were mostly passed in clubs and public houses. In early July 1973 police in Munich arrested five men, including a Briton, and a prominent German lawyer, over a forged dollar racket believed to be centred on London. The ring had put up to seven million worthless dollars into circulation, in various parts of Europe, and this only came to light when banks in Munich and Frankfurt found forged fifty-dollar notes in their foreign exchange holdings. In Munich, at that time, the asking price for notes, which were mostly offered to Americans, was DM 120,000 (about £20,000) for $150,000 (about £59,000). Shortly afterwards another Briton was arrested in Spain for passing forged peseta notes on the Costa Brava.

These fascinating snippets of information I gleaned from the occasional paragraph in the newspapers as I served my time at Leyhill. I guessed the boys were doing well from the production line I had established with such loving care. But I never realised at the time that the net was closing in.

The raid on Garden Road, I discovered later, followed police observation of two men, who held a number of meetings at Charing Cross Station over a period of weeks. One of them was my protégé Stanley Le Baigue. At their final rendezvous Stanley, then aged thirty-nine, from Petts Wood in Kent, was seen to hand Charles Littledale, a seventy-year-old Londoner who looked older than his years and suffered from arthritis, a package.

Police, who had been tipped off about their meetings by an underworld contact, swooped, and found the package

21

contained 1,000 crisp, high quality, forged fifty-dollar bills. And so the cat was as good as out of the bag, and I was on the brink of stepping into the mess it had left behind; or so I thought.

My two friends were taken for questioning to Bow Street police-station where Stanley, a nervous man with little relish for an altercation, admitted the obvious, told detectives he was terrified of the consequences of his arrest, and asked for protection for his family from underworld associates. He was particularly frightened of "Fred" (not his real name), the London club owner who had provided the cash which enabled me to assemble my den. Fred, who wouldn't hurt a fly unless it flew, had told him that he had once murdered a hoodlum who tried to enlist his club in a protection racket.

The altogether cooler Littledale, who later appeared in court in a wheelchair, denied, like the fine pro he was, knowing what was in the packet Stanley had handed him. A close business associate of Fred, he was also to deny any knowledge of the den in Garden Road. But then Littledale would deny the nose on his face if he owed it money. Police inquiries were nevertheless to show that Littledale, who died some years later in prison, disposed of much of the currency produced on my equipment by Stanley. Inquiries were also to reveal that he ran a street-stall in the West End from which he sold forged currency directly. Littledale, nicknamed "Wheelchair Charlie" amongst the criminal fraternity, was Fred's right-hand man on the sales side of the operation.

Back at Garden Road neighbours, who had, in some cases, not spoken to each other for years beyond the traditional pleasantries, suddenly discovered their mutual suspicion of the Black family over the way it had kept itself to itself and failed to tend the garden. The team of ten detectives, led by Detective Superintendent George Sinclair and Detective Sergeant James Salter, meanwhile completed its three-day recovery operation, which was

John Locke, head of the joint section of the flying squad, and the regional crime squad based at Limehouse in East London. The several tons of equipment removed from my house were taken to Barkingside police-station in Essex, near the edge of the Metropolitan Police boundary, for assessment. With it went a large quantity of virgin paper worth at least £10,000.

The forgeries, which were remarkably free of finger-prints, included Bank of England five-pound and ten-pound notes, plus experimental twenty-pound notes, some of them completed on one side only. The rest of the vast treasury of forged currency, which set the nerves of treasury officials across Europe and elsewhere jangling with a mixture of horror and admiration, included forged Irish five-pound notes, American fifty-dollar bills, French franc notes and Australian dollars, together with Post Office giro cheques and a variety of traveller's cheques.

The whole of Fleet Street, news reporters and feature writers, together with batteries of television cameras, enjoyed the three-day encampment on the pavement outside number twenty-eight, overheating the beer-pumps in the local watering-holes, with their insatiable demands for refreshment, and taking over the public telephone boxes for miles around. While the *Financial Times*, with what seemed to me unusual levity in the circumstances, reported one of its dispatches under the headline "Garden Notes", the other newspapers took the matter much more seriously, chartering helicopters to take aerial pictures of the Black residence (and shed) and persuading the milkman and the postman to pose for photographs as they made their deliveries at the then infamous front door. A representative from the *Daily Express* tried the oldest trick in the book on my wife and, as usual, it did not work. He shouted through the letter-box that if she would give him an interview he would ensure the rest of the pack would lift its siege and return to Fleet Street.

Poor Joan! Mother of my three children, Julie, then

twelve, Tracy, ten, and Ian, nine, to look after while I was inside. A woman of infinite patience and understanding! But she was not too fond of me during those troubled times. My wife was forced to toss money (the genuine stuff) over the fence to a friend who offered to fetch the shopping.

Joan, who was scarcely able to pay the weekly bills despite the vast wealth being created under her very nose, was forced to admit to the friends who telephoned that she had been living with her eyes shut.

On the evening of the raid Joan, a Brownie pack Tawny Owl, had driven the children to a meeting of the Sixteenth Bromley Brownie pack in Saint Andrew's Church Hall, where they spent an enjoyable hour, or two, before returning home at about 8pm. She had scarcely had time to brew a pot of tea when the doorbell rang and she found herself confronted by a team of policemen brandishing a search warrant under the Forgeries Act. With the three children, of whom only Julie knew of their father's whereabouts, clinging to her skirt, Joan watched in disbelief while the police spent the next four hours turning the house inside out. By the end of the third day she would not have been surprised if the officers had produced a rabbit from her winter hat.

A former typist at the American Embassy in London, Joan had always believed my explanation that the house was being used by Stanley in my absence to print erotic magazines. This was scarcely in keeping with her image as a Tawny Owl, she realised, but she had chosen to turn a blind eye to it. Stanley, I had told her, was to be allowed to treat the house as if it were his own.

During her ordeal Joan, who was forty-three at the time, told her friends she could blame no one for mistakenly thinking she was involved in the counterfeiting but, honestly, she was "the world's most naïve, ostrich-like woman" who was bound by the running of a home and a Brownie pack. She knew I was no angel but she never imagined what I'd been getting up to. She had never attempted to look inside the study because that was my private room which I'd used as a workshop since we'd moved in. If she had, she would probably not have recognised what she saw anyway. A scientific instrument-maker by trade, I had always disappeared for hours on end to make the strangest of gadgets. Moreover, I had always encouraged my friends to pop in and make use of the machinery I kept, so she had no reason to think it odd that her cousin's husband was always around. As for the shed, she hated gardening even more than I, so she never ventured in.

Police, who could testify to the family's horticultural shortcomings by citing the burns on their hands and ankles from the prevailing crop of stinging nettles in the garden, believed her explanation.

Joan was of course concerned what the other mothers in the Brownie pack would think of her, especially as the secret of my imprisonment had been broken, but she soon regained her sense of humour after the police ended their occupation. One of the ironies which brought a smile to her face was the reflection that Brownies are taught to be observant and that she was their teacher. The time had come, she decided, to take a train to Gloucestershire to demand an explanation from me of my controversial use of the family home.

I was to sign the visiting-order within a matter of days, anxious that not only Joan, but the children too, should come, even though it meant putting the younger two through an ordeal I should otherwise have preferred to spare them. But my wife was not alone in requiring an explanation of what had been happening during the previous eighteen months. I was more than a little curious about the unexpected amount of forged currency which Stanley had printed while pretending that business was slack.

Time was, meanwhile, passing as slowly as a blocked hour-glass for me. The other prisoners continued to amuse themselves over my predicament, asking alternately when

I was planning to go over the wall and whether I could spare a nine-pound note. But I did not have long to wait before word came that the police wanted to see me.

For reasons I shall probably never know prisoner 384315 was permitted, after consultations between the governor, the police and the Home Office to remain at Leyhill, though I'm sure more than one copper would like to have locked me in the deepest vault at the Bank of England and thrown away the key. The weekly visits to Bristol for my catering studies were allowed to continue, and my tropical fish interests continued to flourish. Perhaps the Governor regarded me as too fine an asset to lose. Certainly he stood by me. I was troubled only by a call from the Chief Officer at the prison who announced one morning that a detective had arrived to interview me.

I had already prepared a defence, of course, and even practised an opening address. It was a choice between that and pretending to slip into a timeless coma. So what was I going to say? The equipment I had bought and assembled was to produce soft-core pornography for dealers in Soho, and I had only just bought the paper for the enterprise when I was arrested. Police-officers from Bournemouth, as the Metropolitan Police knew perfectly well, had searched the house when they came to arrest me for passing the stolen banker's drafts and, Heaven knows, looked under every stone. I'd never have had the time, would I, to turn myself into a master forger during the few weeks available to me while I was released on remand from Dorchester before my conviction in February 1972.

Amazingly, though, I was never called upon to present my defence. Instead I tried an opening gambit with the Chief Officer. I just told him that I did not wish to speak to the waiting detective. Miraculously that turned out to be the end of the matter. I was never called to account for the unusual activities at Garden Road. I suppose the police realised they would be torn to bits in court if they tried to touch me for it. Nevertheless, the Home Office appeared to take a precautionary revenge by ensuring that I serve another fourteen months at Leyhill when I had thought myself certain of earlier parole.

Stanley and "Wheelchair Charlie" spent long hours assisting the boys in blue with their inquiries and nearly six months elapsed before they were sentenced at the Old Bailey on January 7, 1974. Charles Littledale, who formerly ran a greyhound-tipping business in Maddox Street in the West End, continued to deny the colour of his socks throughout his trial. The truth, though, was that he had actually allowed me and our criminal associates to install the counterfeiting machinery originally at his own premises for trials before I had it moved to Garden Road. But the court was never told that. Charlie had at the very beginning of the enterprise been made to believe that the machinery was intended to reproduce soft-core pornography but when I felt he was safe enough to be told its real purpose he rubbed his hands and looked upon it as a grand scheme which would add a new dimension of comfort to his wheelchair existence.

At Leyhill I scrutinised the daily press reports of the trial and discovered I was implicated in some of the evidence, but my good fortune continued to hold.

Poor Stanley and "Wheelchair Charlie" were each sent to prison for five years. Stanley had pleaded guilty to conspiring to commit forgery and utter forged documents; Littledale had pleaded not guilty. Stanley also admitted possessing 1,003 forged United States fifty-dollar bills; Littledale not guilty to possessing 1,000 forged fifty-dollar bills. They were specimen charges of course.

Detective Sergeant Salter told the court that Stanley had seemed genuinely frightened of other criminals when arrested. At the centre of his anxiety was a man known to him as "Fred", a big-time club owner and a violent man who was wanted for questioning in connection with a murder inquiry. The court was never told Fred's real name.

Mr. George Shindler QC, Stanley's counsel, said his

client had become a skilled draftsman for a firm of heating engineers but after two nervous breakdowns had fallen under the spell of (wait for it) Charles Black. Apparently I was supposed to be the one who had suggested Stanley could earn big money by assisting me in various projects and who had taught him the forger's skills. I had then, the court was told, introduced him to Fred and Littledale. By threats Fred then persuaded him to help produce the counterfeit currency.

"Wheelchair Charlie", who was nothing if not consistent, denied knowing the machinery at Garden Road was being used for counterfeiting, or that he knew what was in the package Stanley handed him at Charing Cross Station which led to their arrest.

Charlie's performance in court was by all accounts as fine an example of stonewalling as any executed on the cricket pitch by Trevor Bailey. As for Stanley's exhibition of family loyalty – well, I've said it before, you can't select your relatives.

So far as I was concerned the whole experience was of inestimable value. Though I made little money out of it, the venture at least confirmed to me the value of my own skills. The experience, in fact, proved to be my apprenticeship in the art of printing money. After exercising restraint for a couple of years following my release from prison, I again threw the dice in a calculated second bid for instant wealth. But before I turn to that, let me explain how my interest in the art arose in the first place and how I developed the skills with which I have been blessed.

2

It was late October, 1971. I remember distinctly, not because I have a good memory for dates but because most of the children in the neighbourhood were building bonfires in their back gardens, dropping lighted bangers in the school dustbins and lighting up the night sky with the occasional early rocket. My partner, Stanley Le Baigue and I were making our own bonfire in the wilderness of the back garden of my house in Garden Road. I remember I was at the far end gathering leaves with a rake under the oak tree and fetching them over in the wheelbarrow to the incinerator which I had bought and installed a few yards from the back of the house.

To all intents and purposes burning garden rubbish, we must have looked quite seasonal that misty afternoon, and if the neighbours could have seen over the brick wall at the top end they might have been relieved that I was at last trying to do a Percy Thrower and put my three-quarters of an acre into some kind of order. Stanley and I were anxious to look as natural as possible that day but the season of mists and mellow fruitfulness was about as distant from our thoughts as Bromley must have been to John Keats when he wrote his ode to autumn.

The two of us were feeling about as conspiratorial as Guy Fawkes and his friends. The fallen leaves were just a cover. What we were really burning were counterfeit 100-dollar bills.

To print the perfect note with the right tones and tints at 133 dots per square inch, complete with all the images we know and worship, the respectable forger has to run the paper through the offset litho machine seven times each side, before he guillotines it and adds this or that final touch. And the first few sheets have to be adjusted with the greatest care at every single stage. So you might be able to imagine how much painstaking practice and how many frustrating mistakes we made on paper which I was, anyway, not intending to use for the final perfect run.

This meant Stanley and I were lumbered with bags and bags of waste paper which were not simply worthless, but highly incriminatory, and which had to be disposed of. No matter how overwhelming the refuse which the forger produces – and, believe me, it is a major problem – he can't just leave it out for the dustman to collect. So that's why Stanley and I decided to burn our rubbish in the back garden. Now the Royal Mint treats its waste with almost as meticulous a level of security as it does its finished bank notes. But my partner and I, inexperienced as we were in October, 1971, unhappily failed to estimate the care required to dispose of ours.

We discovered to our cost what must be obvious to the average arsonist – when you place thick wads of paper on an incinerator they just glow like logs and refuse to burn properly, so, I found myself a poker and started to stoke the paper to produce the right draught. After a minute or two the fire was blazing merrily enough to burn Rome, and I left Stanley to guard the incinerator while I retired again to the end of the garden with my wheelbarrow and rake in order to keep up the autumnal pretence among the leaves.

It was at this stage I realised various sheets of carbonised paper were floating aloft like black butterflies in the breeze. I leaned against the rake, more concerned than anything else, at that stage, that the oak tree shouldn't go up in a puff of smoke, and scrutinised each drifting sheet to ensure it wasn't still alight. Then to my consternation, after watching one piece flutter through the branches and land at my feet, I discovered I was looking at the blackened but perfectly intact face of Benjamin Franklin. The hundred-dollar bill was entirely recognisable to my well-trained eyes, and I felt as if I were staring at the negative of a ghost. No doubt as white as a sheet, I looked at him. And Franklin looked back.

Stanley and I roamed the garden for goodness knows how long after that, stamping like tribal dancers on the ubiquitous image of Franklin and praying that none of our counterfeit currency had floated over the wall to the surrounding gardens. Fortunately it rained that night, which pleased none of the kids preparing their bonfires for Guy Fawkes night but delighted me.

The lesson I learned that afternoon, of course, was that the only safe way to dispose of unwanted paper is to shred it meticulously first and to place a piece of gauze on top of the incinerator before striking the match – unless you can bribe a dustman with the biggest Christmas box of his career.

I knew rather more about the art of counterfeiting in those very earliest of days than the average layman who thinks a forger's den is run by criminals in green eyeshades hanging wet fivers from a length of string with their wives' clothes-pegs. But I was nevertheless still a novice at many aspects of my trade. Successful counterfeiting requires not only skill, patience and a great deal of capital to buy the range of complex machinery which is the forger's stock-in-trade, but an intense appreciation of security. The average thug who robs an elderly lady or a Post Office needs to be careful only while committing the act. The counterfeiter must be cautious every minute of every day because his premises, if discovered, are as tell-tale as his finger-prints but a million times more difficult to conceal.

The popular image of the forger driving from his suburban home on a dark night to a lonely farmhouse to burn the midnight oil is of course absurd. He would stand out like a sore thumb to anyone with a pair of eyes. I had my den at home because security is a twenty-four-hour a day matter and it is wiser to be constantly on the premises than off.

The counterfeiter must appear to conduct himself like any respectable member of society, blending into his environment like an animal in the field and leading an otherwise blameless life. Criminal he may be, but he never succumbs to the temptation of receiving stolen goods like other branches of his fraternity for that would be to run the risk of inviting police inspection of his home. He ensures his wife is not a shoplifter nor his son a cannabis smoker for the same reason. He does not annoy the neighbours with loud parties (nor complain about theirs) and he doesn't inspire an unwelcome visit by local council inspectors for infringing the planning laws by building an unauthorised extension to his kitchen. The counterfeiter's home is, more than any other Englishman's, his castle. Security of premises – from inquiring policemen to the gasman who has called to read the meter – is more important than the money he is printing even, because without security there would be no money.

The sensible counterfeiter is also wise to refrain from passing a forged note in pub or shop because to be stopped for doing so is to invite police inquiries and so put his whole operation at unnecessary risk. The forger must dispose of his crisp and entrancing product through no more than one or two buyers in large quantities at tremendous discounts. And he must ensure his customers are sound villains who won't drop him in it if their collars are felt by the law. They might sell at twenty per cent of face value to smaller dealers and so on down the line when he has received only fourteen per cent. But the sensible forger regards that as none of his business.

His only concern must be to perfect his product, which means he may be certain to receive no complaints from his buyers, and to ensure his den is as safe as the Bank of England.

I learned the tricks of my trade very quickly in my early forties – late in life perhaps but then, looking back, my earlier years proved the perfect foundation for such a career though I did not know it at the time.

My father, an electrician from Peckham in South London, was quick to realise, bless him, that while I was less than inspired at school by poetry and English history, I was extremely good with my hands and when I was twelve he had the perspicacity to buy me a lathe which I revered as much as I would have the secret of life.

So while other kids with hands like bunches of bananas spent their time scrapping in the local recreation ground, the young Charlie Black put his craftsman's fingers to work making fancy fruit bowls and delicate chess pieces with his absorbing new toy.

Both my mother, who was a hairdresser, and my father wanted me to become an engineer or an instrument-maker so after I had returned from wartime evacuation in the sticks, they enrolled me as a paying student at the Borough Polytechnic near London Bridge to which I took like a duck to water and obtained a very useful first-class diploma in applied mechanics.

By the time I had completed my education I had also developed a talent for taking anything apart – cameras, tape recorders, watches, my Aunt Henrietta's mangle – and putting it back together again, blindfolded. I was also, though I hate to be immodest, a rather fine amateur photographer. So, confident that I could make or repair just about anything metal, I took a job as a tool-maker's improver at the tender age of seventeen and learned how to make press tools which, of course, are used to make a million of the million and one bits and pieces which surround our exciting lives.

I thought my technical training, which was to prove so useful to me in later years, would come to a halt when at the age of eighteen I started my first stretch in one of His Majesty's institutions shortly after the world regathered at the end of the Second World War. Aircraftsman Second Grade 3101794 Black began two years and three months

(I don't know why it is but I always seem to serve a little longer than anyone else) national service at RAF Henlow in the exhilarating county of Bedfordshire. I was expecting little more than a tedious stretch of square-bashing but emerged in 1949 as the camp's Sergeant Bilko.

An instructive time it was to prove, and I certainly emerged a better man for it. In fact I'm grateful to the Berlin airlift, that desperate time when every serviceman too young to have served in the war was bemused by the prospect of having to defend the enemy whom older comrades had fought in another conflict, for extending my stay at Henlow by three months. I learned how to use every piece of equipment in the camp tool-room from a Capstan lathe to a power press and to make everything from a left-hand tap to a right-hand thread. Furthermore, the handsomely equipped facility enabled me to make a fine living on the side – not just for me, but everyone from the friendly flight-sergeant who was responsible for it, down to the men who swept the floor.

Recruits were ordered to choose between becoming millers, grinders or turners upon entry at RAF Henlow, the only metal trades they had there. The tool-room was generally barred to everyone but a few experienced tool-makers and fitters. But with my exceptional aptitude I soon managed to work my way into the inner sanctum, and learned precious lessons which advanced my understanding of the tool-maker's skilful trade.

Now, I remember there was a permanently greasy sort of chap called Bennett in Naylor Road, Peckham, near my parents' home, who ran a workshop in which he sold some marvellous vintage motor-bikes. One weekend when I was home on leave, not long after starting national service, I called in to see him. His wonderful machines fascinated me. It was that visit which turned me into what you might call an engineering entrepreneur. Poor old Bennett was bemoaning the fact that in those impoverished days immediately after the war he was having as much difficulty obtaining new gears to put his bikes back in working-order as the average housewife was having getting hold of surplus ration-books. It didn't occur to me at the time that with a little ingenuity I might be able to forge ration-books. But something else did.

I offered to rebuild and re-cut his decrepit gears for him. There were five or six AC2s working in the tool-room at Henlow, all of them, like myself, proficient in making gears and all of them wondering where they were going to find the money for their next packet of cigarettes. So, with a sorry set of gears complete with teeth as worn as most people's great-grandmother's stuffed into my kit bag, I returned to camp that Sunday evening fired with a new purpose in life.

With the full approval of the flight-sergeant, whom I suitably rewarded for keeping a look-out, I duly re-cut and rebuilt Bennett's ancient set of gears and pocketed the princely sum of six pounds when I returned it to him the following weekend – about double my RAF pay. At the same time I picked up another worn set of gears and, in no time at all, I was running a production line.

The immediate post-war years saw the development of ball-point pens. We take them for granted now but in those days they cost the average working-man a week's wages and they weren't half as attractive or efficient. Furthermore you had to take them back to the shop to be refilled. I like to think that with the assistance of the tool-room I helped in their development. In order to make them I had to help myself to lengths of half-inch ebonite which were locked in the bonded warehouse at the camp, drawing them out stealthily through the wire cage in which they were kept. A little design flair and the ingenuity to make a left-hand tap meant that at the end of the day most people on the station possessed for a mere fifteen shillings a rather sleeker model of the pen than could be bought in the shops for many times the price. Between us the lads and I at RAF Henlow managed to market the product sufficiently well to pay for some of the little luxuries of life normally denied to servicemen.

Officially during my national service I was a miller working a milling-machine making chassis for the radar department, but that isn't quite how my twenty-seven months in the RAF worked out. Good years they were. I'm a firm believer in national service for building a young man's character. It can be a lot more exciting than making an honest living.

The next few years found me working as an instrument maker in the engineering trade during which time I developed an interest in tropical fish. It's said that if a man sits watching a tank full of fish, instead of the television, often enough he'll live longer because his heartbeat and bodily functions will slow. I'm quite sure that's right, but for me the best therapy for stress is to make a living from what you enjoy. I enjoy tropical fish (not least because they don't answer you back) and I did find a way of making money from them for several years.

The inadequacy of thermostat and heating systems at the time inspired me to invent a revolutionary system for tropical fish tanks. And so at the age of twenty-one I sold my precious Vincent HRD motor bike for £285 and put every penny into buying machinery to manufacture the system. My understanding parents allowed me the use of their front room to install a press, bench-drill, guillotine, vices and production lathe, though at one stage their floor collapsed under the weight. Business boomed and I employed several people including Joan, then a secretary at the United States Embassy in London, to help me in the venture during the evenings and at weekends.

In the end the business was getting too big for my parents' house so I moved to behind Forest Hill Station, renting premises, the front of which I converted to a pet shop and the back I used as a workshop to make the thermostats and heaters.

After three years of damned hard work I had saved

£3,000 but in 1959 I sold the shop when I discovered a rather easier method of making a living – buying and selling cars from a site off the Old Kent Road in South London. This was at a time when hire purchase restrictions were lifted and finance companies were falling over each other for business. So I made a small fortune with various partners and expanded to three sites in the process. The success of the business allowed me to buy the land – an apple orchard attached to the property next door – on which I built the family home in Garden Road, Bromley.

But the motor-trade was also to be my downfall. I was sold a couple of dodgy cars, without realising it, by another dealer and in an attempt to recoup the money I lost, I was unwittingly trapped in a racket which had nothing to do with me. I found myself accused by the police of ringing cars and a year later I was sentenced to two years in prison, half of which I served in Wormwood Scrubs, for receiving. Now second-hand motor traders command about as much sympathy in society as bent politicians so I shan't ask for yours. But I was absolutely furious because I was innocent and amazed at being convicted – though probably not as much as my wife Joan whom I never told I had been charged with the offence. The first she knew of it was when a friend approached her to break the news while she was on holiday with the kids at a Butlin's camp on the South Coast.

Not only was I furious but boracic, and I knew that on release I would probably find myself unemployable. But every cloud has a silver lining. At the Scrubs I met three counterfeiters. I knew as much about printing money at the time as an elementary John Bull kit might allow the average child. But thanks to Prisoner 888 White, whom I first became aware of through my duties as a landing cleaner, and two other men who had developed a neat line in printing banker's drafts, I became fascinated by the idea of emulating them.

Prison is the most informative of places, especially for

the novice criminal, because crime is the principal topic of conversation. And prison society is fascinating. It is well known that sex-offenders are the dregs of that society. By comparison counterfeiters are the *éminences grises*. They are held in high esteem by the run-of-the-mill thug for their subtlety and intellectual superiority – qualities which allow them to make a living with their brains instead of their fists. I, who was both furious and desolate at my unjust incarceration, after what had been a blameless life until then, soon realised that with my record I might be forced into crime upon release and it was to the criminals who used their loaves that I was drawn.

No one was cheeky to "Treble Eight" White. I can't say I ever learned a great deal from him about the art of counterfeiting because he had an uncanny knack of being wise without imparting his wisdom. But he set me thinking. I got to know him during association in the evenings, when the other prisoners were generally wasting their time playing cards or snooker.

White was serving eight years for forging company cheques with the assistance of an accomplice in the Post Office. His GPO associate would intercept mail containing crossed cheques drawn on the accounts of big companies and pass them on to Treble Eight. White would then photograph the cheque in question and forge an uncrossed version of it using a letterpress technique in a small lock-up which he rented as a workshop. The wicked fellow would then make out the forged cheque in favour of himself for a cautiously modest amount of just under £1,000, dress up in a bowler hat and pin-striped suit, and present himself with the open cheque for payment at the bank where the company, normally a multi-million-pound concern, kept its account. If the teller showed any inclination to leave the counter to verify the authenticity of the cheque Treble Eight would judiciously disappear.

Like the wedding-guest transfixed by the tale of the ancient mariner, I would sit and listen to the stories he told but I could never persuade him to describe his printing techniques, because he said he was self-taught and that the information was a trade secret.

Sitting at a meal table which included seven murderers he was for me by far the most tantalisingly interesting of all the prisoners in the Scrubs.

White had, however, been caught and his arrest was due to a silly error unconnected with his counterfeiting enterprise. A mix-up over his workshop rent-book led an estate agent mistakenly to believe he was in arrears. Checks were made into his references when the inquisitive estate agent could not find him, these were found to be bogus, the police were called – and poor Treble Eight was nicked.

I learned two lessons from his arrest. Firstly it confirmed my suspicion that all estate agents should be hanged, drawn and quartered at birth. More importantly I realised that the forger, more than any other variety of criminal, is prone to the errors of others. The vital importance of security dawned upon me. The good forger is the one who is meticulous in all things. White put himself at risk by renting his den instead of installing it at home. Moreover he should never have exposed himself by appearing in person at banks with his own counterfeit products. I was not to know at this time that I would meet up again with Treble Eight in prison years later. Then it was I who was to tantalise him with stories of my own expertise. For, by comparison with me and my exploits, White was no more than a gifted amateur in the art of forgery.

The respect accorded to my friend Treble Eight by prison officers and fellow prisoners alike, was similarly given to another pair of fine characters in the Scrubs – Froggy and the bank manager. Froggy's friend was actually the under-manager of an American bank in London and both men were interested in improving their standard of living.

A book of specimen banker's drafts, which was kept at the bank for the use of staff, proved to be the key to their quest. The drafts, which were the genuine article, were bound together in this book but had heavily scored "specimen" across them. Most importantly they indicated the signatures required by bank officials for the issue of the drafts – the larger the sum, the higher the seniority of the signatory. To know what signatures were necessary on what amounts and to have genuine examples of them was to have the keys to Fort Knox as far as our intrepid friends were concerned. Banker's drafts, which of course cannot be stopped once they have been issued, are every bit as good as cash in the forger's handbook.

Froggy's banking friend kindly lent him the precious book of specimen drafts when a safe moment allowed him to do so. Froggy recruited a photographer – actually an old boy who had spent his working-life as a printer and who was similarly interested in improving his quality of life – and, bingo, they were in business. After printing some high quality forgeries of the borrowed drafts and adding all the right aforementioned signatures, they fetched an associate over from Germany, dressed him up in square steel-rimmed spectacles and a Tyrolean hat, and despatched him round the capital collecting money, which he did as nonchalantly as a bus conductor taking fares. If they hadn't been so greedy I don't think they would ever have been caught. Froggy's friend's bank started to get suspicious at the large holes in their reserves and that was the end of the game for them.

Stories like theirs fascinated me, and the possibility of a whole new way of life slowly opened its doors. After six months of the finest education an incipient criminal could ask for, I was transferred to Ford open prison, in Sussex, to finish my sentence. Now Ford is paradise compared to the Scrubs, but I found myself feeling cheated of the company of such interesting members of society. One meets the cream of the criminal fraternity, care of Her Majesty's penal institution in West London and none is quite so refreshing as the company of counterfeiters. I envied their skills. My appetite was whetted. I resolved to become one of them.

My first stretch inside ended in September, 1969. But my determination, upon breathing the wholesome air of Bromley again, after my release, to build a forger's den and print my own money had to be set aside for a while. That, I knew, would take a long time even if I could accomplish the task. I was meanwhile desperately strapped for cash and needed an instant infusion of the stuff. Sex, or rather other people's diverse range of interest in it, proved to be the answer. Unemployment was the alternative.

To cut a long story short, I borrowed a pile of money from Ned Bridges, a friend in the car game, gave my parole officer the slip for a few days, and caught a plane to Copenhagen. There I rented a cheap basement office where I hired a pretty girl to help me handle some mail which I knew would soon start arriving in torrents from England – once I had got a rather simple money-making scheme off the ground in London.

I devised a less than honest organisation called the Scandinavian Film Club, specially designed to cater for the secretive sex needs of the British. I didn't feel proud of it at the time and I don't now. But needs must when the Devil drives.

What I did back in London was pay to have printed a rather explicit but confidential batch of questionnaires inquiring about people's sexual needs on writing-paper with the club's name as a letterhead. Then I compiled and printed a complementary list of bogus hard-core Scandinavian film titles designed to suit people's individual needs. I advertised the Scandinavian Film Club in girlie magazines, circulating in London, and invited readers to apply to the Copenhagen address which I had set up with the girl for their questionnaires and film list. As I had anticipated, the applications arrived in the Danish capital as fast as clothes falling off a troupe of overdressed strippers.

41

Lisa, the girl in Copenhagen, and I got to work processing them all and sending off the questionnaires and film list. I had taken care in the small print on the questionnaire to point out that when requested films were out of stock I would send equally satisfying films instead, which I considered catered to their stated preferences. Meanwhile I had bought a large stock of cut-price soft-porn movies from an acquaintance in London at about five pounds for a 200 foot, eight millimetre film as well as a large quantity of jiffy bags.

It all worked like clockwork. After our bumph had been posted off to all the greedy applicants (you'd be surprised at the voracious appetites of all manner of respectable people) Lisa received about 5,000 deeply moving replies requesting films which would have made her blush if they had ever existed and posted them to me at an accommodation address in Piccadilly, London. They were all, as I had hoped, stuffed with money. I posted off the innocuous soft-core films in the jiffy bags, accompanied by a note explaining that the requested film was out of stock. I don't suppose Lisa received more than a dozen complaints in Copenhagen, which she posted on to me. People who buy plain-cover pornography through the post prefer not to stand in the witness box and be cross-examined over their replies to a personal sex questionnaire. I had known all along that I should be immune from arrest for lack of available evidence.

The enterprise allowed me to pay back Ned Bridges and left me with enough money to keep the wolf from the door for several months while I turned my attention to more lucrative and challenging matters.

3

It was not until a year had passed that the opportunity arose which allowed me to bite the bullet. I bumped into an acquaintance – a chap with a large pocketful of traveller's cheques which he had stolen from the firm of security printers where he worked. They were the genuine article and had a face value of about £200,000. Was I interested in selling them? I certainly was. But to whom?

Ned Bridges, the motor-trade friend who had lent me the readies to finance my Scandinavian Film Club enterprise, was the brains behind a rather lucrative greyhound-tipping business in Maddox Street, near Soho, where he was in partnership with Charles Littledale ("Wheelchair Charlie") and the gaming club owner known as Fred.

Discretion being the greater part of valour I shan't disclose Fred's identity, not least because he knows how to handle a gun and might not be pleased with me. Anyway, I decided that Fred (for that was the name given to him by Stanley Le Baigue at his Old Bailey trial three years later) might make a suitable customer for the stolen traveller's cheques so I duly presented myself in the West End with a few crisp samples of the merchandise.

Fred wasn't often given to smiling, but on this occasion he afforded me a glimpse of nearly all his gold teeth. He said he needed a day or two to make inquiries about where he could place the whole £200,000-worth. But, unfortunately, by the time he rang me back and I telephoned my supplier from the firm of security printers, the traveller's cheques had been snapped up by someone else. It was then that Fred, who knew my credentials and my ambitions through Ned

Bridges and who was also aware of my manual adroitness, made the fateful suggestion – "Why don't you print some yourself? If you reckon you can do it, we'll set you up."

That was exactly the sort of proposition which I needed, of course, but I was sensible enough to be cautious as I really didn't know whether I had the talent. But I agreed to take some time off to find out.

In America, it is said, if you have the brains you can learn how to construct a nuclear bomb through freely available papers in many of the major libraries. I don't know if that is possible in Britain. But with the right ability to interpret what you are reading you can certainly teach yourself most of what you need to know about the printing techniques necessary to counterfeit the currency of good living.

So I spent the next two weeks at various libraries in London preparing for an O-level in forgery. I've never been a great reader, but I do enjoy peace and quiet so I felt at home in the reference sections pouring over dozens of technical books and printing-trade magazines from early morning to closing time. In fact I was so enthralled by the precious material in front of me that if the silence had been broken by a nuclear bomb under the table at which I studied, I probably wouldn't have heard it.

I'm a quick learner and during that fascinating period I saw the same flash of light which must have illuminated Archimedes (he's the man who discovered a method of detecting the amount of alloy in the crown of the king of Syracuse and I'm sure he would have made a wonderful counterfeiter). The *eureka* sensation pursued me for the month which followed my dizzy course of study. During those four weeks I graduated to A-level counterfeiting. The gods must have been smiling on me because at that time there were huge simultaneous exhibitions at Olympia and Earl's Court of lithographic, letterpress and photographic equipment. I wandered from stand to stand pestering the lives out of just about everybody involved in the graphic and photographic arts. But of course every salesman and technician in sight was only too pleased to demonstrate his equipment.

Fortunately photography had always been a hobby of mine. I could dismantle the most complex of cameras and put them back together. So that side of my education in counterfeiting, which is a complicated mixture of skills, came easily. Printing was a different matter. When technicians at the exhibitions I visited dropped subjects like colour separation, hairline registration and screen clash into our conversations I moved my brain into another gear and listened hard.

My next task was to draw up a shopping-list. The items I needed weren't the stuff you could buy at Sainsbury's – cameras, plate-makers, inks, paper, a guillotine, a letterpress printing machine, an offset litho press, amongst so much more. Where was I to buy it all, for how much, new or second-hand? Which equipment was compatible with other equipment and which kind was better than another? These were some of the questions which took me from manufacturer to manufacturer. So, for instance, at Gestetner in Tottenham Court Road, I'd be found making up my mind to buy a 212 offset litho machine, but not the same manufacturer's light boxes, cameras or plate-makers. My weeks of painstaking research had taught me I could buy better elsewhere.

None of the manufacturers lost patience with me because they knew by then that I knew what I was talking about. Some of them, though, could be a bit inquisitive about what I wanted this or that for. My well-rehearsed explanation was that I represented a firm of wholesalers, large, but not top-notch, which wanted to print its own catalogues to cut out the expense of contract printing. We required top quality reproduction of manufacturers' bumph in our own format and we were expanding fast enough to need to develop our own print-shop. That was the story I gave to anyone who asked.

My scholarship and window-shopping complete, I returned to talk business with Fred. Now Fred is a gentleman, in the criminal fraternity, but you don't mess around with a man with a reputation for refusing to be bullied by Kray twins or murder squad detectives alike.

It might have been Fred's idea to set me up as a forger but then Fred likes to be careful with his investments. No one with any sense would want to put them at risk if he valued his person. So, believe me, when I went back to see him early in the summer of 1971, maybe two months after his original proposition, I was very careful to be sure I knew what I was talking about.

Fred listened without interruption in his jaw-clenched way to my assessment of the counterfeiting business and said: "OK, we'll back you. Go shopping."

I was given a blank cheque (yes, a real one) to buy all the equipment I needed and at the outset it was decided we should install it at the greyhound-tipping premises in Maddox Street where there was spare accommodation. We knew we would have to move it to another site later, so the manufacturers and distributors, and the police, for that matter, would be thrown off any scent which we gave off. But, in the meantime, I could use it as a perfectly legitimate enterprise and practise anything I wanted, in order to perfect the techniques necessary to graduate to forgery. Charles Littledale had a sufficiently clean background to obtain credit for those more expensive items of equipment which we preferred to buy on hire purchase, and he held the lease on the premises in Maddox Street. The only problem was that Fred wasn't sure Wheelchair Charlie would appreciate having his perfectly respectable premises turned into an incipient forger's den. So we decided to concoct a story which Charlie would swallow.

In those days the shops in Soho which specialised in selling hard-core pornography were having a lean time importing their material and were constantly losing it in police raids. So we put it to Wheelchair Charlie that we wanted to install the equipment in order to reproduce, regardless of the Scandinavian copyright, some of the more liberal-minded girlie magazines from that frozen region of the northern hemisphere (I've always thought it curious that the colder the climate, the greater man's prurience – perhaps it's the fault of their women). My own experience with the Scandinavian Film Club came in particularly useful in persuading Charlie that I was familiar with the market demands. But Charlie, it turned out, needed no persuading. He thought it such a wonderful idea that he insisted on introducing me to several of his acquaintances in the porn trade who were desperate for material. In fact they placed with us an initial order of 1,000 front-to-back pirate copies of a warm-blooded magazine which would have given Mary Whitehouse apoplexy.

None of us was in the least bit concerned about copyright infringements because it was felt that the source of the pirate copies would be virtually untraceable, and the whole venture seemed so feasible that, for a while, I wondered whether we shouldn't give it a try especially after we had bought about £1,000 worth of glossy paper from Gestetner, useless for currency counterfeiting, in order to convince Charlie further that we meant business. The equipment necessary to reproduce pornographic magazines is identical to that required to counterfeit currency. Only the potential rewards and penalties are different.

So that was that. With butterflies performing the tango in my stomach in the summer of 1971, I awaited delivery in Maddox Street of the complex machinery I had ordered from a score of manufacturers.

But, in the meantime, I'm afraid that, due to the hole in my wallet, I had foolishly set a time-bomb ticking at the threshold of my career as a forger. After the Scandinavian Film Club affair I devoted the first half of 1971 to satisfying my thirst for invention. As an instrument-maker I have always been fascinated by mechanical challenges. Stanley Le Baigue was a heating and ventilation engineer at the time. With his ability to identify a market need, and my mechanical inventiveness, we developed a revolutionary, cheap pipe coupling system for the plumbing trade. That done, I went on to design a "dye-alarm" for people in the security business, which emitted an indelible dye to help identify an assailant. Finally, I developed a device for blowing up Christmas balloons for people with no lungs. But none of these inventions earned me a brass farthing, such is the lot of the inventor. So, not for the first time in my life, I found myself strapped for cash.

The light-fingered friend who stole the traveller's cheques from the firm of security printers which employed him, had earlier proved to be equally adept at helping himself to some banker's drafts from the same generous source. I started to get on very well with him. He knew all about letterpress printing at a time when I was anxious to learn all I could about the craft, though his knowledge of the more complicated art of offset litho was poor.

He had a knack for pilfering so-called machine waste from his letterpress which, any security printer will tell you, should have been shredded.

Some sheets of double-error stamps, which the Crown Agents were producing for I forget which outpost of the Commonwealth, once found their way into his pocket. They were only imperfect, however, because he chose to print them imperfectly. In his experienced hands they were so valuable they might have knocked the philatelic world off its axis had the stamps found their way onto the market. For my friend had managed to acquire them before the final printing processes which would have given them their fourth, and final, colour and before the sheets had been perforated. Unfortunately for him they proved too hot to handle.

On the other hand, the banker's drafts which he offered to me early in the summer of 1971 would have been approved by the chief cashier of the Bank of England. In the machine-shop where sheets and sheets of them are produced, the final stage of printing is their numbering. This is performed by a device called a numbering box which, in principle, is a bit like a mileometer. Numbering boxes have a habit of failing to turn over in sequence on occasions and when one box fails the printer stops the machine and pulls out the imperfect sheet. This machine waste should then be shredded and burned. But my friend wasn't fond of destroying valuable items.

He offered them to me to sell elsewhere but, boracic as I was, I decided to pass them myself with the assistance of a friend, Ben. A sunny day on the South Coast at Bournemouth, Brighton and Worthing followed. But while most of the other day trippers were queuing up to buy ice-creams and soft drinks, Ben and I were inspecting the goods in all the better jewellery shops.

I have always felt jewellers to be amongst the greediest members of society and when Ben and I made it plain we had an awful lot of money to spend on diamond rings the chaps we did business with that day seemed to throw caution to the wind. Perhaps it was the combination of our good manners and the crispness of the banker's drafts which threw them. But, whatever the reason, Ben and I departed the South Coast with their best thanks and about £5,000 of sparkling gems. When it came to selling them for cash in London later we got rather less than their face value of course but the business, like the Scandinavian Film Club venture, kept me in funds during the time I was researching the art of counterfeiting.

As I immersed myself in my studies I forgot all about that trip down the A23 and it was not until six months later, in November 1971, that the police caught up with me. Though I had often sailed close to the wind before and was indeed in the throes of pulling off a major criminal enterprise, the deception on the South Coast was actually my introduction to crime – I had been innocent of the alleged car ringing which put me in prison the first time. It had been a simple, and skilful, sting and probably the finger would never have been pointed at me if Ben hadn't been nicked for something else later on. In return for a bail guarantee which the police dangled over his nose despite his criminal record, he dropped me in it.

The result was that Ben, with seventeen previous convictions, got eighteen months for deceiving the worthy South Coast jewellers while yours truly, with just one previous conviction, was sent down for five years at Dorchester Crown Court in February, 1972. I was of course fortunate that, as I have described, the swedes (that's what the criminal fraternity, as well as the Metropolitan Police for that matter, calls the rural boys in blue) failed to discover my forger's den at Garden Road when they came to arrest me. But I still felt a bit miffed at the prospect of losing half a decade of my liberty. Judges really should get their act together and sort out a uniform sentencing policy, not least on the South Coast where the spirit of Judge Jeffreys seems to have survived the past 300 years.

With the six months' time-bomb of my misdemeanour there ticking merrily away, I meanwhile awaited delivery of my counterfeiting equipment at Maddox Street where, incidentally, there had been a couple of changes in personnel. Ned Bridges had fallen out with Fred and Charles Littledale, and in fact never had any further connection with the counterfeiting operation. Stanley Le Baigue joined us.

Now Stanley was a good ideas man but he knew nothing about printing. After our time together earlier in the year when we failed to market my plumbing and security inventions, Stanley was out of work and embarrassingly boracic. He knew I was up to something because I kept having to travel up to town, and, when he inquired about the nature of my business, I told him he shouldn't be interested because it could lead to trouble. But he said he was skint and didn't mind taking a risk. So I told him I had been asked to do some printing without letting on exactly that I planned to put the Bank of England out of business. As the days went by and I gradually let on a little more he begged me to include him. I explained that the people with whom I was involved were professionals and difficult to get in with. But in the end I told Fred and Wheelchair Charlie that I needed an assistant and when I vouched for Stanley they agreed to cut him in.

Poor Stanley was to tell judge and jury at his Old Bailey trial in 1974 that I had pressured him into joining the partnership. This was nonsense. Stanley enjoyed a fat living for eighteen months, while I was serving time at Leyhill, printing piles of counterfeit currency at my house on my equipment which I had taught him to use after he had volunteered for the job. But I have never picked him up on it since. What you decide to say in court is as much your own business as the secrets you tell a priest in a confessional.

Stanley actually proved to be a quick learner and a competent forger (after all, he had a good teacher). Like me, in the early days of our operation, he expected to make a nice living out of counterfeiting but never the millions which represented the face value of the notes which rolled off my press.

His only failure, and it was a big one, was his imperfect understanding of the need for absolute security. Once, at the very start of our operation, he had his car stolen from outside his house. Unhappily the boot was crammed with tins of magnetic ink, plates, negatives and, most importantly, about $500,000 worth of American one hundred-dollar bills printed only at that stage on the back. How we recovered the vehicle (or rather how I did because Stanley was too quivering a wreck to do anything about it) after enlisting the help of the police is a hair-raising story which I'll amuse you with later.

It took about three weeks during that exciting summer for all the equipment I had ordered to be delivered to Wheelchair Charlie's premises in Soho. The second-floor offices were quite spacious, and, by pushing and shoving the filing cabinets and furniture around, we made enough room to take delivery. Unfortunately, though, the staircase was narrow and winding so I anticipated one hell of a problem in getting some of the bulkier machinery installed, not least the offset litho which was virtually the key to the enterprise.

Initially the plan was to winch it from the delivery vehicle to the office through the window but the traffic disruption which would have arisen in Maddox Street from the crane, which we would have had to hire, was something which could not be contemplated. The offset litho weighed something over six hundredweight and stood about seven-foot high. So Gestetner decided to deliver it in pieces.

The jigsaw of components which arrived took three men two days to put together again. Naturally I was more than a little keen to watch them assemble it, knowing that mine would soon be the task to take it to pieces once more and reassemble it at Garden Road. Unhappily the men did not share my eagerness that they should communicate their expertise to me. Whether they were trade unionists, I don't know, but they certainly seemed to believe in a closed-shop. I tried as airily as I could to suggest it might be helpful to me to observe them in case I should ever need to move the machine elsewhere. But amid a sharp intake of breath their foreman told me not to dare even think about such a thing. In the first place, he said, that would neutralise the guarantee and secondly only God and he were capable of such a task. I retired to another part of the building feeling about as apprehensive as all the king's horses and all the king's men sifting through the pieces of Humpty-Dumpty.

Two days later I inspected the assembled machine and for just a brief moment wondered whether it might not be more sensible to run the counterfeiting operation from Maddox Street. But the constant clatter of feet on the stairs as people entered and left their offices above and below ours reminded me that the security there was about as leaky as a colander. So I told myself that if Gestetner could do it so could Charles Black.

By the end of the third week everything else had arrived too, including the bulkier objects like the plate-maker, the drying cabinet, the sink unit, guillotine and camera. About three weeks after that I opened the door to three men from a removals firm with whom I had arranged to have the equipment transported to Garden Road. They looked about as puzzled by their task as the men from Gestetner would have been if I had asked them to reassemble a pile of furniture. On the floor were boxes of nuts, bolts, washers and gears which once held the offset litho together, accompanied by the disassembled skeleton and flesh of the machine. Yes, I had managed the easier half of the task, though my colleagues in crime were muttering that I'd need the assistance of a magician to put it back together at home. The Incaf camera was also in bits as, it appeared to them, was the whole counterfeiting venture – not to exclude Fred's financial outlay. Now everyone knows that what goes up must come down. Charles Black also knows that what comes apart goes back together again. Having had the experience of taking everything to bits I knew I'd be able to follow the original formula of construction.

I told the removal men we were moving offices but had to put all the equipment into temporary storage at my house. So off we went to unsuspecting Bromley where the heavier machinery was reunited with the lighter stuff which I had already taken home by car.

Everything was stored in the double garage at home, for a further period of three weeks, while I constructed the shed in my garden which was to form one half of my den. It was in the shed that I reconstituted the precious offset litho in just one afternoon. So much for the Gestetner foreman! The chainpile delivery was one tooth out. I had not realised the gears were marked with stars and they had to be assembled exactly in order for the paper to go through the machine properly. That was my only mistake and I very quickly rectified it. When I then found it worked correctly Stanley Le Baigue, who had stood anxiously by all afternoon, was amazed.

The twin sites of my den were fully assembled, like Creation itself, in a week, and for the following three weeks I experimented with a sense of enthralment which few people are ever fortunate enough to experience.

4

It was a happy family photograph, of which I was particularly fond, showing my kids sitting on Father Christmas' knee in his grotto at a London department store, which I selected to practise my incipient skills as a counterfeiter. A good clean picture, it had lots of different colours and was nice and sharp. Taken the previous Christmas, it showed the man from Lapland in white beard and red tunic trying to look avuncular with the sweat running down his face and my three offspring clambering all over him, surrounded by toys. You know the sort I mean. My task, on which my future depended, was to reproduce it in halftone on fine art paper with a million and one dots in all the right places, identical colour to the original, and perfect smudge-free definition.

After ten days' trial and error, working round the clock at times, I presented the finished product to Fred at Maddox Street. I felt rather like a schoolboy who knows he's come top of the class handing his school report to his father. Fred inspected the copy and the original side by side. The look of this hardened criminal smiling with pleasure at the two identical pictures of my family at play with the patron saint of children was as bizarre as it was rewarding – though I'm quite sure that in the place of Father Christmas, Fred saw instead the image of Her Majesty the Queen, or some other head of state, who graces a bank-note. This colourful beginning was proof to him that the man in whom he had invested so much money had the skills at his finger-tips to copy items of great value, even though he had an awful lot still to learn.

I shall explain in detail the various processes which went into the making of my Christmas *tour de force* as I go, the mastering of which allowed me to tackle traveller's cheques – the next stage in my career – and currency. The methods, which were at times hard-learned, apply to them all.

In a nutshell, we're talking about a handful of fundamentals plus a host of specific procedures, according to the task in hand, with which I shan't risk cluttering your understanding at this stage.

Firstly, I photographed the Santa picture on a process camera, making four negatives of the original. This I did through special filters in front of the lens to separate the four primary colours of the original from each other. Next, I exposed positives which I had made of these through screens on a plate-maker to make four metal printing plates, one for each colour. This process converted the image from continuous tone into dots as numerous as the hairs on your head for half-tone printed reproduction, such as you find in a high-quality glossy magazine. Then I attached, in turn, the four plates to a cylinder in the offset printing machine, the workings of which I shall come to. Finally I ran the glossy paper which I had bought through the machine four times, applying four different inks to build the picture stage by stage. I had already perfected, of course, the shades of the ink after complicated experimentation.

If you think all that sounds straightforward, then read on; but read on anyway even if you don't. Believe me, when I was first researching the theory, and trying to work out a system, I was sometimes as bamboozled as a choirboy at a Wild West poker table.

First of all, I bought some best quality glossy paper, reams and reams of it actually, because I knew I'd have to do an awful lot of practising. It was obviously only later that I had to select paper carefully, and treat it, to match the currency I counterfeited. At this stage, of course, Charles Littledale still thought my purchases were for reproducing pornography. And, incidentally, it was also then that Ned Bridges decided to pull out of the operation over a business dispute at Maddox Street, and he took no further part. With my equipment in place at home I began the task of becoming a forger.

The four primary printing colours, all present in the Father Christmas photograph, are black, yellow, cyan (blue) and magenta (red), and I had to make a colour separation of these. You see, to print in colour you actually have to run the same piece of paper four times through the machine, once for each colour. And you must allow each application to dry before applying the next, though a special powder is used to help because art paper doesn't allow ink to dry by absorption. You have to print one ink on top of the other and whatever printing machine you use must have hairline registration so that the colours of the finished product have perfect definition.

But I'm jumping ahead. In the first place I had to photograph the Father Christmas four times, making sure it was in exactly the same position each time. The negatives had to be punched so when I put them together, each with their individual colour, on a pin bar they would be identically placed, one on top of the other. A pin bar is just a device to ensure perfect registration. It was essential to the work and one of the many features of my beautiful camera.

The camera was a treat to get to know, except that we were, of course, labouring in a room crammed with equipment which had to be as black as a Newgate knocker. So Stanley and I constantly found ourselves performing a *pas de deux* at the most inopportune moments. Thus it was that, to overcome the difficulty of our enforced blindness, I bought some luminous paint from a joke shop and marked the corners of the camera, the sink, and just about everything you can think of.

One problem for which there was no solution, however,

was the heat and glare from the four 500-watt tungsten halogen lamps. One second we were in darkness as black as midnight and the next as brightly lit as the lamp of God. I would have to close my eyes and count perhaps ten seconds by the white dots which swam in and out of my brain before I could open them again.

Tea and sandwiches kept us going through the long hours of day and night. But we were sustained by something else as we worked, which was good for our self-confidence. We knew that, in the unlikely event of a tap on the door by the police, they would find us up to something for which they could not touch us. Time and right were on our side while we were merely practising at being forgers with a Father Christmas photograph. To have started experimenting with something incriminating like a banker's draft or a traveller's cheque would have been to take an unnecessary risk. Nevertheless, the dark room remained locked at all times and the children were kept away by my wife who believed, though scarcely approvingly, that I was about to start reproducing pornography.

Having to photograph the same picture four times, once for each colour, in exactly the same position and perforate them, will sound easy enough to anyone with a decent understanding of the subject. But one or two things had to be overcome first. Not least of these was that I had to make a filter-box. It was to take gelatine filters for absorbing the light of the other three colours, as I made negatives of each of the four primary colours in turn, in the Father Christmas photograph.

Now, during my shopping expeditions for all the equipment I knew I would need, I bought a densitometer which is a photographic instrument for measuring the density or opacity of negatives. More precisely, it measures the density of emulsion on the negative. No, not the matt, gloss or silk stuff with which you cover the ceiling and your tit-for-tat when the wife orders you to stop watching the snooker on the box and get on with the decorating. It's the light-sensitive layer of chemical compound suspended in gelatine used to coat film, which "holds" the image taken by the camera. The densitometer was to prove invaluable in ensuring that the ratio of incident light, and that emerging from a photographic density, was within the right range for my purposes. I quickly learned that if the densitometer showed the density to be wrong I had to allow longer exposure or a longer time in the development, depending on which end of the range I needed.

My training as an instrument maker had meanwhile assisted me in making the filter-box – a round disc about the size of a dinner plate with holes cut round the periphery. The gelatine filters, which must not be touched by hand, I then slotted into the disc apertures so I could turn them round, as necessary, to place them in front of the camera lens in order to perform the colour separation. Experiment taught me how long each of the four filters had to remain in front of the lens as I took the four shots of the original photograph in order to blot out the unwanted three colours at a time. I found I needed perhaps five seconds with the one colour I wanted to remain per shot and perhaps ten with the next as I made my four negatives. The lightest part of the negative, and the darkest, needed to be within a certain range on the densitometer. And when I came to develop each shot I had to use a stop-bath and a clock with a bell to ensure I didn't under, or over, develop.

My trials with the densitometer, the filters, and the development to ensure I got everything right, took me four days of patient hard work. That period included learning how to master the use of a screen – the next stage in the counterfeiting process. The screen is the transparent plate containing a special optical pattern for converting the four, single-coloured, continuous-tone Santa photographs into a series of dots for making my half-tone reproduction.

The screening process meant that I was left with four printing plates, each with 133 dots to the square inch, which, when put on the offset litho would produce a printed image guaranteed to deceive the naked eye into believing it was looking at a continuous tone picture. Only under an eyeglass could the dots, overlapping or side by side, be distinguished. If you look through the same eyeglass at, say, a five-pound note you will find that it is continuous tone. There are, of course, many dots in the picture making up the Queen's face for example, but continuous lines such as the Duke of Wellington's tunic and the lettering itself really are uninterrupted.

The way the genuine article is printed is by photogravure, a process by which a sunken engraving is made on a metal plate from which ink reproductions are made. It is a completely different process from the one I was developing and it is employed, I think, not just to try to defeat the likes of me, but because of the tremendous printing runs the Bank of England requires. Unlike this hardy animal, the plates on an offset litho might give you only, say, 100,000 copies at very best, and a smaller machine scarcely more than 30,000 before you need new plates. It doesn't take long to make new plates, but the old lady of Threadneedle Street can't be messed about like that.

So what the Bank does is have a highly-polished cylinder on a huge printing machine from which you wouldn't get much change out of a fortune. On it are the lines of the note etched at different depths which determine how deep or thick the colour is on the note, so you may have two lines of the same thickness but varying in depth. Because ink can do funny things on paper, according to the depth at which it is used, the colour turns a different hue. All this, you will understand, is second-hand information because the old lady has never invited me to inspect her printing processes – anymore than I would have welcomed her to Garden Road.

The feel of the five-pound note is partly due to the thickness of the ink which is raised in part. You can actually pick it off with a pin. Now the raised effect isn't important to the look, but without it, the note might feel odd. When I came to print currency I continued to use the offset litho and, by that process, the ink goes on as flat as a pancake. The result, which was fine for Santa Claus and indeed the traveller's cheques of the day, was a terrific appearance but a feel which left something to be desired. I had to simulate the raised effect but I shan't describe how at this stage. I had many techniques ahead to master as I neared the completion of the pre-printing stage of the Father Christmas picture.

On the fourth day of my amateur beginnings in the summer of 1971, I took myself to the shed, armed with the four plates – six thousandths of an inch thick in aluminium – which I had made on the plate-maker from the set of colour-separated negatives. It was a proud moment.

There was a cosier feel about the shed than the hot and airless darkroom which I had nicknamed the submarine. For a start there was a comfortable smell of ink and cedar, more in keeping, I suppose, with traditional notions of the atmosphere of a forger's den. My arrival did not mean, however, that I was home and dry without problems. The greatest difficulty was getting the colours right. Regardless of the excellence of the offset litho it would only print in the colours I poured into the ink duct, and whoever heard of a Father Christmas in a pink tunic? Such an effect is possible if you forget you are printing in half-tone because you are in fact mixing coloured dots with the whiteness of the virgin paper.

The consistency of the colour is equally important, especially when you're counterfeiting currency. Compare several copies of the same colour supplement of a Sunday newspaper and note the variation in colour. That standard is not acceptable when you are getting down to reproducing bank-notes.

In the shed, which externally at least would have done Percy Thrower proud, began the second half of the operation. Using many hundreds of sheets of paper in all, I put about fifty at a time through the Gestetner machine and used about half a dozen settings of ink from faint to heavy on each batch. Each was carefully marked and filed. This I did with all four colours.

Like a good housewife, I would wash down all the equipment – though in my case, with white spirit – between applications of the four different inks. As I advanced from colour to colour, and plate to plate, and ran the same partially printed sheets through the offset litho to build a complete picture, I learned that the equipment had to be spotless. An overlooked spot of black ink from one run can make an awful mess on yellow when you turn to that colour.

The colours had to be applied exactly on top of each other finishing, sensibly I thought, with the black. And it was here that the punch holes I have already described answered the demands of hairline registration. It was only after a great deal of experiment, using all the different ink settings of all four colours, that I was able to sort out the right combinations to allow me to proceed.

The only serious trouble I had was with the blue. It was simply too blue for what I wanted, even on the lowest setting and, at first, I could not understand why. But I worked out there had to be something wrong with the negative, which meant I had to return to the darkroom and check it with the densitometer. This told me I was too far up the emulsion range, so I had to endure the performance of making another negative within the range and a fresh plate, and put it through another screen. It was quite a performance and, for a while, blue ceased to be my favourite colour.

The ultimate test of colour matching, with the Father Christmas photograph, was whether my eyes told me everything was right, and that is a perfectly good method. But nowadays a forger may save himself this eyeball-aching business by using a colour scanner, costing another small fortune. A set of colour separations can be his in ten minutes and he can be certain they are perfect. I hesitate to say that with technical advantages, such as this, counterfeiting today is easier and therefore more prevalent, but back in 1971 a good forger was a rare creature. This was not just because of the expertise required; so much steady patience was needed, and this was simply beyond normal people.

Thus it was that ten days after embarking upon this crucial experiment in forgery, regularly working from 9am until 3am the next day, I was left with an identical copy of the photograph printed in half-tone on shiny art paper. How did I feel? Like a cat which had broken into a dairy. I realised the system could be beaten. By Charles Black Esquire! The limited exercise which I had completed told me everything I wanted to know. It was the living proof of my skill, and I could not wait to make a fortune from it. Up to that point everything had been theory alone. The practice was something quite different.

The scarcely disguised manic expression in his eyes as Father Christmas contemplated the pleasure of stuffing my kids up the chimney was to me quite beautiful. And for its perfect reproduction I had to thank the jewel in my collection of counterfeiting equipment – the offset litho. I don't know how many years a young printer's indentures or apprenticeship lasts these days. However long it is should be regarded as a mark of the complexity of the trade. So, in introducing you to the offset litho – which was about as important to me as the Black Prince's balas ruby is to the Imperial State Crown – I do not expect instant comprehension.

Without going into fine detail, this is how it works. Just think of your grandmother's mangle and it should help. There are three cylinders – plate, blanket and impression cylinders by name – plus two ink rollers and a water damper. The metal plate containing the half-tone, or dotted image, made from the photographic negative, does not actually touch the paper it is printing. The thin plate, which is about fourteen inches long by about ten inches wide, is wrapped and secured round the polished plate cylinder.

The material the plate is made of, and the way the image is imposed and fixed upon it, mean that the image areas alone are receptive to the ink. As the cylinder revolves with the plate attached, it is fed by three rollers. One is a water damper, a long roller with a felt cover, which absorbs water and in turn keeps the plate moist. Then there are two ink rollers, fed by adjustable ducts, which brush the plate as it revolves. The ink cunningly congregates on the image areas, while the rest of the plate remains clear of it. The inked image is then transferred from the plate cylinder onto the revolving blanket cylinder, which is also made of metal but is covered firstly in canvas and then in stretched rubber about a quarter of an inch thick. On the plate the image is the right way round but on the blanket it is received in reverse – like the image of newsprint in a mirror. The blanket cylinder in turn revolves against a clear, plain impression cylinder. And between these two cylinders is fed the paper, like your grandmother's bloomers through the mangle, which receives the inked image proper. So all the wear and tear is taken up by the rubber blanket. Thus it is not direct printing of image onto paper but offset, from which the name of the process is derived. Clear as mud? Fine.

After bagging the mountain of waste paper, non-incriminatory of course, and removing it to the local tip I travelled in high spirits to Maddox Street to show the fruits of my labours to my partners.

Normally a man of grunts and nods, Fred was as effusive as a Mafia boss at his daughter's wedding – beaming upon my family as if it were his own. He knew what I had been working on, though I hadn't previously shown him the original photograph, and had agreed I should be left alone to practise my experiment. Fred had shelled out on everything from the shed to the camera, having had the perspicacity to realise he could be on a winner. So he shook me warmly by the hand instead of by the throat. I was saying, quite euphorically, "It's a piece of cake," and he was saying, "I knew you could do it, Charles." If I had known then the hurdles I should have to jump to turn his delight into hard cash, I think I might have been a little less relaxed. After all, what stage had I reached in mastering the art of counterfeiting? For me to take it on was a little like saying to a man found sweeping the road: "Right, you're intelligent enough. You're going to set aside your broom, clean yourself up and learn to be a brain surgeon."

Charlie Littledale, who still believed my Santa photograph was a practice run for a venture into the sleazy world of pornography, was also pleased, though he might have wondered from the Yuletide evidence I produced whether my work would be sexy enough for the demands of the market. But he was on the point of having his illusions broken. I waited, with some trepidation, for his reaction as Fred told him: "Now look, Charlie. I'm afraid we can't for the moment lay our hands on the right sort of pornography for Charles here to reproduce. It would be a shame for him to lie idle until it turns up, wouldn't it? So what I have in mind – and I think Charles is agreeable, aren't you, Charles? – is for him to reproduce some traveller's cheques. What do you think about that?"

My apprehension proved to be entirely misplaced because Wheelchair Charlie immediately took to the idea like a seed to soil. He said: "Why didn't we do this in the first place? It's a much better idea!"

Charlie was a wealthy man in his seventies, severely crippled but with the brain-box of a man half his age, and the last thing he needed to do was take the risk of going into counterfeiting. His priority, I suspected, was to free himself of unnecessary hassle during his declining years, so it was rewarding, in a way, to discover that the old man still had a taste, not just for the loot, but the excitement the winning of it brought.

The adrenalin certainly coursed through yours truly as I left Maddox Street and turned to the more interesting

65

phase of counterfeiting traveller's cheques. Posing as a man about to take a holiday, I took myself, and my passport, to a branch of Lloyds in the West End, where I acquired something like £200 worth of fifty-pound cheques and £100 pounds worth of twenty-pound cheques, which were clipped into a booklet in the usual way. Of course, the heart-breaking trouble with this little exercise was having to sign each one in front of the cashier, knowing that I should soon have to face the hassle of erasing my moniker from them when I came to counterfeiting these handsome little fellows. Either I had to reproduce unspoiled, virgin forgeries or everyone in the criminal fraternity who bought them would have to change his name to Charles Black! Not good for business, that.

Even more problematic, however, was the acquisition of a numbering box – you remember, those small printing machines with numbers embossed on a series of wheels. Without a numbering box I'd have been forced to counterfeit the traveller's cheques with the same numbers as the originals from Lloyds, a silly risk. I managed to make a box for myself when I later came to counterfeit United States dollars but at this stage of embarking on my career I did not know how to, not least because I did not have one to copy.

The numbering of my forged traveller's cheques would, I knew, also have to be in magnetic ink for this specialised substance was part of the banks' electronic numeral recognition system. Yes, all those funny little fat figures at the bottom of every cheque, which you can never be sure you've read correctly, would head straight for your little boy's toy magnet like iron filings, if they had the energy.

How was I to overcome these annoying difficulties? Well, I called in some specialist help. You may remember my saying that before I took up counterfeiting I had been offered some genuine stolen traveller's cheques by an acquaintance who worked for a firm of security printers and that I offered them in turn to Fred, but by the time he decided to take them they'd already found a buyer.

It seemed to me the time was ripe to recruit this enterprising person to our fold. In first planning the counterfeiting operation with Fred I had told him that really we were likely to need another hand. So I went to see the boss again and told him we should deal the fellow in. He might not know a thing about offset printing, I said, but he was an expert at letterpress, a method of relief printing in which the type stands above the areas of the printing forme. Rather more importantly he could steal from his employers those vitally important numbering boxes which, of course, you couldn't just go out and buy in the High Street. My sense of security and my professional pride would not allow me simply to reproduce the booklet of traveller's cheques, numbers and all.

Defensive about his profit margin, Fred prevaricated for a while about the extra cost of taking on another man and we discussed the possibility of simply buying a numbering box from him, but that would have meant he would have had a shrewd idea of what we were up to. In the end I convinced Fred that bringing him in was more advantageous than not and when I contacted our prospective new partner he was delighted to give a hand. With him he brought three electronic numeral recognition system boxes and other numbering boxes for which we might have a need later on, together with a supply of magnetic ink, though it was possible to go out and buy that. Jolly useful too the man turned out to be at a range of work, turning up to help on a Saturday or Sunday for a few hours, and maybe one evening a week when his job at the security printer's allowed him.

Following exactly the same procedures which I had developed to reproduce the Father Christmas, I began work on the fifty pounds Lloyds traveller's cheques, though this time there was a lot less trial and error. But after photographing the original I had to attend to the removal of my ball-point signature. This was a pain. It could not be washed off because the ink would have smeared and there was no way the difficulty could be resolved through working on the original. The answer lay in the negatives. This time, instead of making one set of four negatives for each of the different colours of the original, I made two sets.

To cut a long story short, I solved the problem by excising the portion of one set upon which I had signed my name, and superimposing another matching portion – whether it be filigreed or clear – which I had cut from the other. I'm quite sure I'd be a good wig-maker. By the time I'd finished fiddling around with the negatives to make them signature-free, no one could see the joins. I used a fine surgical knife for the job and the same implement to touch up the emulsion where the superimposition had created a few dots a bit too heavily. The same technique was used to delete the numbers at the bottom of the cheques.

From that point it was plain sailing. From the negatives, their superimposed section sunk beautifully into place. I followed established procedure to make four plates and took them to the shed to print the forgeries. This time I knew exactly how ink behaved and thus how much colour to run.

The paper, which I again ran four times through the offset litho for the four primary printing colours, presented no difficulty. Choosing it had been a little like buying wallpaper. I went to several manufacturers and merchants, asking to inspect swatches – books of samples. No one could tell the difference between the paper I eventually chose and the paper from which the traveller's cheques were made. At home I had a micrometer with which I measured the thickness of the originals at four thousandths of an inch, though paper is actually produced and sold not by thickness but by grams per square metre, according to its density or compression. I selected a standard paper of about seventy-five grams per square metre, which was, incidentally, identical to the thickness of the cheques.

Quite frankly it did not need to be of the finest quality though I had to ensure it had no manufacturer's watermark for obvious reasons, and there were probably five or six types available which would have done the job just as well.

It is actually the feel of the paper which is of paramount importance, regardless of its thickness. You find, when you get to know paper a bit, that you can pick one type which is thinner than that of the original you are reproducing but, because it is stiffer, it feels thicker. Reproducing the feel of a bank-note is, of course, of inestimable importance to the forger with any degree of pride in his work but this is rather less the case with traveller's cheques. I suppose that, while people are relatively unused to the feel of traveller's cheques, they have a pretty shrewd idea of how a bank-note should feel. Most people know the silky feel of the note between thumb and first two fingers and will often hold it to the light to check for watermark and metal strip. I shall leave the question of choosing paper for forging bank-notes, and treating it, to give it the right feel until later – as, indeed, I shall keep you in suspense about the strokes of genius which allowed me to overcome the problems of watermark and metal strip. Suffice it to say, at this stage, that the forger needs paper of the finest quality for printing bank-notes. A note gets folded, and unfolded, I don't know how many times. I have seen some bad forgeries – not my stuff of course – and they have virtually torn in half after a couple of foldings, because the paper is of such poor quality. Never spoil a good job for the sake of a halfpennyworth of tar. Your customer isn't likely to come back if the notes you sell him fall to bits in his back pocket – unless to wring your neck.

I said, a while ago, that everything was plain sailing, but there were obviously complications which we had to take in our stride. For one thing, unlike Father Christmas photographs, traveller's cheques have perforations, and they come complete with a card cover in booklet form, don't they? Banks have a high-speed paper-drilling machine to make the perforations, which I did not possess, and did not wish to buy, just to enable me to counterfeit a couple of thousand cheques or so.

I bought some perforating strip with exactly the right number of perforations to match those on the traveller's cheques, which I mounted on a punch-and-die machine I had made in my workshop. On the basis that one hole in a piece of paper looks much the same as any other of the same size, I shan't weary you with further description of that part of the exercise. As for the card cover, which also required two holes – well, I could have printed that with my eyes closed. In fact I may well have done, so knackered was I at the end of ten hard days in my forger's den. I printed about ten covers at a time and bought some clips for the binding together of the finished product.

More of a nuisance than a complication during the printing stage was the washing up of the ink. If anyone fancies designing a dishwasher to do the job he can count on me as his first customer. I used to run the heavy colours, the black and the blue, on one removable head – the set of three rollers in the offset litho – and the light colours, yellow and magenta, on a second head. This reduced the washing up and the risk of fouling say the yellow with an unnoticed blob of black.

Complete with my new partner's magnetic ink numbering, the traveller's cheques I forged were excellent, astoundingly so. I hate to be immodest, but no other words describe them. The banks had a special security recognition machine in each branch which they would use, when they chose, to ensure the cheque registered correctly. And the magnetic ink was the key to the reading. It seemed to be the only obvious control on authenticity they employed. As far as I am aware, every single one of my precious little fellows passed with flying colours – I never heard of anyone having to leg it out of the bank with the cops in pursuit.

Magnetic ink is just like the ordinary stuff but with iron

particles thrown in. Each cheque was numbered individually and by hand by a letterpress process not dissimilar to a John Bull effort. The numbering box, provided by my partner and central to the operation, automatically changed the numbers in sequence. But it needed manual intervention when I wanted to change to a different sequence every fifty cheques or so. The numbering box and the Adana letterpress worked hand-in-hand. I used a chase to hold the former in place and a platen or metal sheet to hold the forgeries and press them against the numbering type. It was just a question of pressing a lever up and down; the ink rollers went over the numbers on the numbering box and the Adana pressed them against the cheque.

Every single forgery was printed individually on a sheet of A4 paper and trimmed by electric guillotine before being christened with a number. At a later stage though, when I was printing dollar bills, I did three to each sheet. There is no justification for throwing away good money when paper is so expensive.

The final variation from my original work on the Father Christmas photograph involved the rubber stamping of each cheque with the name of the issuing bank branch. This was on the front. On the back, which was otherwise blank in those days, was another stamp listing the countries which would accept the cheques. These were stamped on as the customer collected them. In my den I had an engraving machine and I was able to make, without difficulty, my own rubber stamps from a quick-setting compound like an epoxy resin. The engraving, of course, had to be done in reverse. Not wishing to make a fortune out of one particular branch I made several identification stamps representing a variety of branches.

So there you have it – the Charles Black version of printing your own traveller's cheques, all in ten days. My rapid mastery of the art, however, was not the only reason for the speed with which I delivered the finished product to Maddox Street. Within a day or so of starting work

I received a telephone call from Fred saying he urgently needed to see me. When I arrived in Soho the big man told me we were in trouble. To my dismay he explained a rival operation was in the very process of offering him – yes, forged Lloyds traveller's cheques. For a moment I felt like Captain Scott must have, on finding Roald Amundsen's flag at the South Pole in 1911, though my language upon discovery was probably worse than his. Fred said my competitor's product was almost ready and that from the sample he had seen it was passably good. How long would mine take to deliver? he asked. I made a guess, subtracted my grandmother's birthday, and told him one week.

"What I'm going to do, Charles, is this," said Fred, anxious to protect his investment in me but no doubt unhappy about turning down good business from another source. "I'm gonna give you the week. And I'm gonna hold the other man off till then. I'll tell him what he's doing could ruin us."

How Fred used his influence to persuade the man to hold off is none of my business but suffice it to say I pulled out all the stops to deliver fast. A little while later I heard my rival had been nicked. He was apparently at Heathrow Airport when he got stopped with the plates, forged traveller's cheques and goodness knows what else. What the circumstances were, I haven't the faintest idea.

A week after our meeting, I rendezvoused with Fred in a hotel in the West End, taking with me a mixture of the original traveller's cheques and my forgeries. Fred took them into the toilet and when he came out he wanted to double-check with me, which were which. It was my pleasure to show him. Amid the back-slapping which followed from the other boys, I felt pretty damned pleased with myself. I had taken to the art of counterfeiting like a duck to water on a rainy day. Whether the banks would also fail, like Fred, to tell the difference between butter and margarine I had no idea.

In fact they, and everyone else to whom they were passed never had a clue what had hit them. I printed something like £250,000 worth and I think well over half were cleared before the whistle blew. I'm sure it was only the flood of them in a short period in Central London which alerted the banks.

Fred had a handy network of Fagin's helpers in the West End, little gangs of three, or four, waiting for deliveries. There must have been up to ten groups and they split Central London into areas or manors, never trespassing on each other's territory. The big man would say: "OK, here's £10,000 or £20,000 worth of cheques. You go out and do them. We want back a third of the face value and any unused cheques." They all went to work like beavers.

Forgers don't take holidays, except of course when they're enforced by the courts, so with the plaudits of my colleagues still ringing in my ears I began counterfeiting Barclays and Midlands traveller's cheques in no time, my techniques guaranteeing perfection. We were printing everything to order, and didn't care what it was. Fred got the orders and called the shots.

I was never caught but the end of the game came quickly, I remember. One day I went out to buy some traveller's cheques, I forget from which bank, and I couldn't get any. It was as if the fifty-pound cheque had gone out of fashion overnight. No branch in London had one. Once the banks collectively discovered there were forgeries in circulation they raised the alarm and withdrew the genuine article. They had to be redesigned to thwart the mystery forger and, needless to say perhaps, when they re-emerged some months later, they were not lacking in improved design complexity. In the meantime the average traveller and the honest counterfeiter were offered traveller's cheques in denominations which were not worth the effort of copying so far as yours truly was concerned.

Reproducing traveller's cheques in the names of all, or most, of the clearing banks kept me in employment for little more than a month, though it was a well-paid occupation while it lasted. Why did it take so long for the banks' alarm to ring? Well things were a little technologically slower in those days, so rapid has the computer revolution been. The cashing branch returned the traveller's cheques to the issuing bank after checking that the numerals were in magnetic ink or telephoning to check the number had been issued if the cashier were suspicious. In those days, so far as I could tell, these were the only means available to confirm authenticity. So it was generally not until the cheques were received by the issuing bank that it could begin to be apparent that hundreds of thousands of pounds' worth were not all they seemed. It took three days before the issuing banks received them. It meant a three-day safety margin for the likes of Fred and me – but, of course, seventy-two hours as a potential minimum for the banks to discover they had been defrauded, nevertheless meant that traveller's cheques have a notoriously short shelf-life for the forger. It was only because of this that I realised I should accept the greater challenge of counterfeiting currency which has a incomparably longer shelf-life.

The only traveller's cheque I distinctly remember not attempting to reproduce was the Thomas Cook variety because they were specially embossed – an art form I was not to learn until later in my career. But I was particularly pleased with one other variety I produced in the name of a New Zealand bank. The boys chose to pass them on a day when there was a bank holiday in the faraway south Pacific and there was absolutely no means for even the most suspicious of Cockney cashiers to check their authenticity. An awful lot of villains hit dozens of banks in London that day.

So I quickly ran out of work with traveller's cheques, having gained the distinction of getting ahead of the market and ruining it. But in the pipeline was an American dream. Fred heard from someone who wanted United States dollars. That was my next task.

5

A sense of security should be instinctive to the successful forger and I always tried to instil in my disciple, Stanley, the discipline which must necessarily accompany it. To give him credit, the man made few mistakes and was a fast learner. But his one major misdemeanour took years off my life in terms of the nervous energy I expended to correct it. For a while I was nearly as jittery as Stanley was at the best of times. It all went wrong for us in the late summer of 1971 while I was in the process of counterfeiting dollar bills.

Now, in my experience, the time the police are most likely to raid a suspect's premises with a search-warrant is in the early hours of the morning, before anyone but them, and the milkman, are out of bed, and when their quarry is too drowsy to acquit himself like a gentleman. So I continued to follow the well-tried procedure I had adopted during the making of the traveller's cheques. (Incidentally, at the end of that exercise I burned everything which was inflammable, cut up the plates, with other metallic bits and pieces, and turned them into a mulch at the bottom of a witch's cauldron of caustic soda in the back garden.) At the end of a day's work Stanley and I would spend an hour meticulously cleaning up all the machinery. Then we would pack the most incriminating paraphernalia involved in the reproduction of the dollar into cardboard boxes for nightly removal from the premises – the plates, negatives, blanket cylinder (no matter how much that was scrubbed the image of what was being forged would never completely disappear), ink (all shades of green for the dollar), and paper which had already been printed.

Next we would resort to the best subterfuge I could devise to throw the boys in blue off the scent, if they should call unexpectedly. Piles of pornographic magazines were the expedient in question. I'd scatter them all over the place so the police would think I was reproducing them in my forger's den. In the camera I'd put pornographic negatives I'd shot from the magazines and on the offset litho there would be pornographic plates I'd made from them. All right, we would get nicked in a raid and fined under the Obscene Publications Act in all probability. But I guessed the police probably wouldn't seek to confiscate our machinery which they would do for currency counterfeiting because I made sure the pornography was nice and soft, not the really bad stuff. The whole scheme, I imagined, at least gave us a fighting chance.

The cardboard boxes, crammed with all we held most dear, were Stanley's special responsibility at the end of a day's work. We'd pack them into the boot of his pride and joy, a second-hand 3.8 S-type Jaguar for which he'd paid £500, and off the fellow would drive for the ten-minute run to his semi-detached. There he was supposed to secure the unloaded vehicle in his garage, checking the locks and bolts as automatically as breathing.

The thinking behind this security-system was obviously that if ever I were spun by the police they would find not a hint of a currency counterfeiting operation *chez moi*. Having a criminal record – though for something I had not done – meant I had to be particularly cautious whereas Stanley, whose past was as clean as the driven snow, was unlikely to have his collar felt. As systems go, it worked extremely well for months. That is until the night in question.

I remember that for once we called an early halt to the job. Stanley wanted to get away at about 10pm because his mother-in-law was visiting. This may sound implausible,

I know, because most men prefer to procrastinate in the circumstances. Still, that's what he told me, and off he went after we had followed usual procedures. In bed, nice and early for once – my wife must have wondered who I was – I lay awake pondering the problems of reproducing the greenback. They look easy enough, easier than sterling but, believe me, Uncle Sam is no fool because those notes are more ingeniously designed than the security at the Jewel House in the Tower of London. In addition to the extraordinarily elaborate filigree, the lettering on the note is partly in a type of reverse-block design – some letters are white against a dark background, others normal, produced by what I call mixed positive and negative printing. So the photogravure was taxing my counterfeiting resources to the very limit. Nevertheless I had contrived to complete the art work for the backs of the fifty and twenty-dollar bills and I was not displeased with the result.

It was a large, freshly printed pile of about 6,000 sheets of these incriminating little beauties which Stanley was transporting that night to the bosom of his unwitting family. Each sheet contained the unguillotined backs of three notes – one fifty dollar and two twenty dollars. Within hours of his departure from my house I became convinced that in no time at all the rest of the planet would be sharing the secret of Stanley's car boot. Shortly after 9am – the time he generally arrived at Garden Road – my protégé telephoned.

"Charlie," he said. "I don't know how to tell you this. The car's been stolen."

Now Stanley was seeing the doctor about his nerves, but I don't think a large Valium sandwich there and then would have calmed him down. It was probably just as well he was on the phone and not at my front door. My inclination might have been to wring his skinny neck. And I'm not a violent man, you understand. The conversation went something like this:

"What do you mean the car's been stolen?"

"Well," he said, "I'm sorry, but I left it outside the house last night. Like on the road. The mother-in-law, you know, it was so late and I had to drop her off home. I got back about one o'clock in the morning. I just didn't want to make a noise and wake the wife up opening the bloody gates."

"But that's the earliest you normally get home and make a noise, you pillock."

"Yeah, but the wife would just have been dropping off and she doesn't like being woken up."

"What happened then?"

"Well I stuck it outside like I said. I was going to get up in the morning, quickly like, and I never give it a thought anybody would take it. It's the area, you know. We never used to have people like that down our road nicking cars. Sorry, Charlie, what shall I do?"

"God! I can't believe this. You prat! You know what was in the boot don't you?"

"Yeah. What shall I do? I mean I'll do whatever you say."

"Do nothing. Absolutely nothing, Stanley. Wait there and I'll come and pick you up. Then we'll decide what to do. Don't even breathe. Do you understand me?"

Stanley clearly didn't because the next thing he said was: "Shall I phone the law? Tell them it's been nicked? I mean I can't just do nothing."

"You've done enough already, Stanley. Get us into this mess any deeper and I'll probably want to kill you. Pillock!"

"But my wife knows about it and she isn't very happy with me."

"Just tell her to shut up."

The dear lady hadn't got a clue about her husband's occupation since he gave up his job as a heating and ventilation engineer a few months earlier, on account of his nerves. Knowing he and I were working closely together, she must have assumed as far as I know that we were involved in some kind of engineering project, as indeed we had been. Not backwards in offering her opinion on a variety of matters, she would not have been amused by Stanley's means of keeping her – nor by the impending publicity on the use to which the family car had been put. With a hurricane about to descend upon them she had about as much chance of avoiding the scandal as if her nervous spouse had appeared on *What's My Line?*

I picked the fool up without crossing his wife's path and drove him back to my place, my incredulity gaining momentum with every set of traffic lights we passed.

"It's very awkward, Charlie," he said. "You see the wife's already told the woman down the road and her old man's a copper."

"For Christ's sake, will you tell her to shut up or shall I do it for you? Tell her you're going to report it. Tell her you have reported it. But tell her to keep her nose out of it."

I sat the idiot down in my house, fed him with strong, sweet tea, and paced the lounge like a man in a condemned cell looking for the inspiration to escape.

Stanley next said: "What about the insurance on the car? What do I do if we never get it back? If I don't report it that's what will happen. What do I tell the missus?"

"Never mind the bloody insurance. My prints are all over the boot. They're all over everything. The forensic boys will think it's Christmas. You can always say the car was nicked and there was nothing in it when it went. That's your out. You're OK, Stanley. You can look after number one. But what about me? I'm the one in the shit. My prints are already on file, remember? Yours aren't. You're clean, aren't you? You can be the innocent victim. You can say your car was nicked to transport something illegal and it was found with the stuff still in it. It was nothing to do with you, you can say. But what about me? What do I tell the cops? That I was kidnapped and stuck in the bloody boot with all this stuff I'd never seen before? And that's why my prints are all over the place? Stanley, you're going to come out of this smelling

79

of violets if you'll just stop twitching for a minute. But I'm going to smell like last week's dustbin. I still fancy killing you, you know."

Stanley was as nervous and distressed as a headless chicken, and in those circumstances I suddenly realised that the gravity of our predicament was only likely to worsen. So instead of laying into him I decided to keep a cool head and placate the fool. It may have been going beyond the call of kinship but I offered to pay for his car if expediency prevented his making an insurance claim. To a degree that did the trick, relieving him of the spectre of his irate wife.

The first thing we had to do was alert Fred that we were expecting the police to break down the door at any moment and jump on us. The boss had to be warned to cover any tracks which might implicate him. I phoned and gave him an abridged version of our tale of woe before catching a train to town for a case conference that morning. To my surprise what he and Charles Littledale came up with during the meeting was nearly as daft as Stanley's conversation with me in Garden Road, though without the hysteria. Wheelchair Charlie said he thought we should call the police in to find the car. I told him not to be so crazy. Nowadays, with cars stolen every two seconds, the police just phone you up when they find yours. But in 1971 they removed a stolen vehicle to the cop-shop and put a warning sign against it to stop anyone touching before the forensic boys arrived to take a butcher's for any evidence that it had been driven in the commission of a crime. Naturally they would open the boot, and that would mean goodbye Charles Black, unless, of course, I could come up with an impossible fairy story to explain the presence of my prints on everything in the boot and several tons of immovable counterfeiting machinery in my house.

I told Fred and Wheelchair Charlie that it was my freedom which was on the line and to stay well away from me – not even to phone – while I tried to do a Harry Houdini out of my shackles. But not before Fred made an interesting contribution to the conversation. From a master criminal, supposedly cool, intelligent and ruthless, it was the silliest suggestion I had ever heard.

Fred said that in Burlington Arcade, a stone's throw from Maddox Street, he had seen on display several advertisements for a product which he couldn't actually remember. On the front was the advertised product but on the back was a mock-up of a dollar bill.

"Couldn't you pretend, Charlie, if the law opens up the boot that you printed the backs of a pile of greenbacks for an advert for something and you hadn't done the fronts yet? I'm sure we could find someone who'd vouch for you, someone in advertising. I'm just thinking who we've got on our books to do the trick."

"For what and for whom would this advert be?" I protested. "And how would that explain all the secret equipment in my house? The cops know a forger's den when they see one. And you don't need one to print a few adverts, do you?"

"Oh well, just a thought," said Fred.

Wonderfully helpful, wasn't it? I had Stanley worrying about his car insurance, Wheelchair Charlie suggesting I handcuff myself and Fred coming up with cock-and-bull which wouldn't fool Winnie the Pooh. To hell with it all, I thought. This is an exercise in logic and the only one who has any is me.

I went over the possibilities of what had happened. The first was that a gang of professional thieves had stolen the car to ring it, cannibalise it or use it for a job. The Jaguar was a perfect, high-speed vehicle to do a bank job. If they were intelligent then, having inspected the contents of the boot, they could be expected to telephone Stanley to demand a slice of the action in exchange for the counterfeiting equipment. On the other hand, if they were petty thieves they'd take one look at the equipment, panic and chuck it all in a ditch somewhere. That would eventually mean a certain visit from the police. There was a third scenario, however. The car might have been stolen by joyriders and abandoned.

After twenty-four hours had ticked by without contact either from the police or the criminal fraternity I began to feel the third explanation was the most likely.

"We can't just sit around here drinking tea and doing nothing," I said to Stanley. "How much petrol was in the tank?"

Stanley said it was only about a gallon. That meant fourteen, fifteen, sixteen to twenty miles at most before the car ran dry. The thieves had not got keys to the two petrol caps so unless they had broken one of them open to fill up with juice they might well have left the vehicle where it stopped and maybe pinched another one to continue their travels.

That was why that very day I went out to buy street maps of the towns and boroughs around Stanley's home for a twenty-mile radius. No matter how long it took, I decided, my partner and I were going to cover every damned street looking for the Jaguar. But before we undertook our mammoth task it occurred to me there was just one chance of a short-cut. If the car had been illegally parked where it ran out of petrol it might have been towed away to a car pound. So we went to three, at Orpington, Elephant and Castle, and Kilburn, looking over the fence where possible or, when we were forced to present ourselves, spinning a yarn to explain our search – such as, a friend had borrowed the car and left a message on our answer-phone to say it had broken down but failed to explain where – in order not to implicate ourselves in case the boot had been opened. It was a delicate business, and quite fruitless.

So the grinding task of sweeping hundreds of miles of streets, major and minor, began. I drove while Stanley navigated. At times it was as farcical as the plot of a Laurel and Hardy movie: "Another fine mess you've got me into, Stanley!" We covered areas of about three or four square miles at a time, using Stanley's house as the centre of an ever-increasing circle, fanning out into every single road, avenue, lane and cul-de-sac, exploring blocks of flats, council estates and car parks. The atmosphere in my overworked car was less than cordial as Stanley ticked off byway after byway.

At the end of the third full day of searching we had our first break. A woman who lived in a cul-de-sac half a mile from his house telephoned the increasingly bewildered Stanley to say she had found his box of tranquillisers in her front garden among the rose bushes. She'd been in touch with his doctor, whose name was on the label, and obtained Stanley's number.

"I guessed you'd been visiting the area and they'd dropped out of your pocket," she said.

Stanley was able quite truthfully to reply that he had been visiting her part of the world in the past day or two – along with what felt like half of London and the Home Counties.

To me the discovery of Stanley's blasted pills, which he immediately collected, indicated one thing: the thieves, who must have thrown them out of the car window, were aimless joy riders who had no idea where they were driving. Why else should they turn up a suburban cul-de-sac and drive out again? It did wonders for our confidence, even though we knew the pills might have been lying there for three days, and encouraged us temporarily to redouble our efforts. The wheels never stopped turning from eight in the morning until dark for what seemed like another eternity. But I'm afraid we continued to draw a blank. Sick and tired of the whole exercise, I decided the time had come either to break Stanley's legs in retaliation for his stupidity or devise a different strategy.

It had to be admitted that the only people with the facilities and expertise to find the wretched car were the police (I didn't know any spiritualist mediums). But the problem was how to enlist the assistance of the cops without giving the game away. The solution lay in what had been staring me in the face for days: Stanley's nervous disability. The poor fellow leaped like a scalded cat when I outlined "Plan B" to him but the look in my eyes must have told him there was no escape from it. I told him he had to walk into his local police station and say he had lost his memory, not for the first time, and that he suffered from black-outs. Thanks to his condition he had lost his car a week ago. He felt sure it hadn't been stolen; he just couldn't remember where he'd left it. He hadn't come forward for the whole week because he was too embarrassed and anyway he had expected a phone call from friends or neighbours who might have spotted the vehicle.

"I don't want any arguments, Stanley," I told him. "That's what you've got to do."

"I can't do it."

"Why not?"

"I feel so stupid."

"You are stupid, bloody stupid, Stanley."

"They'll never believe me. I've got no chance. I'm not that good an actor."

"You're going to do it, Stanley. You're going to win an Oscar. For me, you're going to be Sir Laurence Olivier, got it?"

I ran over the plot many times with him, impersonating a station-sergeant while he learned his lines. I cajoled, threatened and reassured him. I showed him carrot and stick.

"You're under the doctor and you've got the pills to prove it," I said. "Tell him he can ring the bloody doctor to prove it if he wants. You're obviously stupid, so just be yourself in there. You say you went out one day, you can't remember where exactly. You don't remember coming home or how you travelled, but when you went out again the next day your wheels just weren't there anymore. You say it happened to you once before. But that time you lost your memory only for an hour or so.

You were lucky then because a neighbour had seen you park outside the newsagents and told you where the car was. That's why you're sure it hasn't been stolen this time."

I schooled the idiot until he knew the script inside out and, after a final pep talk, drove him to the police station.

"There's one other thing," I said, dropping him off.

"Yea?"

"You don't mention my name."

I parked the car round the corner, resisting the temptation to keep the engine running. Stanley went in like a reluctant schoolboy to the headmaster's study. When he re-emerged he was altogether cockier.

"I done it," he said. "You'd have been proud of me, Charlie. But it wasn't easy."

"What happened?"

"I spoke to the sergeant like you said. He said 'Pull the other one' when I told him. It took a lot of talking. But I convinced him I wasn't larking around, that I wasn't a loon."

"You must have been good then," I said. "So what's he going to do about it?"

"He's gonna circulate the loss to all the cop cars and everyone on the beat and find the thing for us."

After Stanley's award-winning performance I took him home and returned to Garden Road, keeping a weather eye open as usual for half the Metropolitan Police, whom I constantly expected to find parked outside my house as I turned the corner. Waiting for the other shoe to drop didn't compare to my apprehension that the inevitable was about to happen. I felt we had done all we possibly could to recover the car intact, but I was very pessimistic about the outcome. Five or six years sharing a cell with someone else and his smelly feet seemed to summarise my future, even though Stanley had enlisted the boys in blue to do our work for us.

For a week I had tried to put my affairs in order, telling my wife I might be spending some time away from home and where she would find the money to look after herself and the kids. When I hadn't been driving I had padded around the house, while at night the torture had kept me awake. What I hadn't put Stanley through in the course of those seven long days isn't worth knowing. But I hadn't been home five minutes from the trip to the police-station before my partner was on the phone to me.

"They've got it," he said triumphantly. "They've only found it for us. They've just phoned. The copper on the desk did. The car's at West Wickham. Just down the road. Bloody good, aren't they?"

"We went to West Wickham."

"We must have missed it," said Stanley.

"I realise that, you pillock. What's the catch? What else did they say?"

"Nothing. They just said West Wickham. I got the address. They told us to go and pick it up. The number plate's hanging down a bit at the front but it doesn't look as if it's damaged."

"They were fast finding it, weren't they," I said, betraying my suspicions.

"Amazing! But I don't think there's any problem."

"Did they say how they found it?"

"Some old dear phoned them at the nick a few days back. She said it had been there a while and she wondered if it were stolen. They must have checked it out and found it hadn't been reported, otherwise they'd have belled me, wouldn't they? They weren't perturbed. They just thought it was parked there. I think we're in luck."

"We'll see."

Was it a trick? I kept asking myself as I drove over to his place to pick up Stanley. Better to drive by it first in case it is. It so happened we had actually driven along the road in question – I can't remember the name of the road now – early in our search and if it had been there at the time we must have missed it by a whisker. It was near the periphery of the circle we'd drawn to search, maybe about twenty-five miles from Stanley's house and a bit further than a gallon of petrol should have taken the thieves.

Suddenly, there it was, the elusive beige Jaguar waiting for us as if it had never been away. Or was it to prove a Pandora's box? We drove past it several times, me more nervous than Stanley for once and highly suspicious that the police had already opened up the boot and were waiting out of sight for someone to turn up for it. I glanced through the window as I drove up and down, looking at all the possible places where a surprise party could be in hiding. In the end there was nothing for it, but to take the plunge, so we pulled up behind it, got out and opened the boot, rather like a bomb disposal expert examining a suspicious parcel. No one with a whistle leaped out; everything was still in place as we had stored it. Mafeking had nothing to the relief I felt, but I wasn't anxious to hang around enjoying the feeling and ignored Stanley's inane grin.

One bolt had worked loose from the number plate at the front, which was hanging down and actually touching the road. It had probably been driven over some rough ground. Apart from that, the vehicle was unmarked. After patching up the number plate, and pouring a gallon of petrol into the tank from a can we'd taken with us, we took off in convoy.

When I got home, Stanley immediately behind me, I said: "You are never, ever going to take anything out of this house again, regardless of the consequences. I'd rather have it all here and if I'm busted, then I'm busted. I don't care. At least I'll be able to sleep at night again."

Harold Wilson once said a week in politics is a long time. I understand what he meant. After the nightmare of the previous week I found myself having to rearrange my entire security-system, inevitably compromising it in the process. And I had to really concentrate to get myself motivated again. But the problems involved in counterfeiting the dollar paled by comparison with what had interrupted the work.

I had told Fred, who had received an inviting order for the dollars, that the continuous tone of the greenback would be a challenge but that, in general, it looked easy enough. I couldn't have been more wrong and I must confess that while I was working with Stanley, for Fred, I failed to perfect the forgeries. They were good, don't get me wrong – up to ninety per cent on a scale of excellence and they fooled the banks – but short of the ninety-seven per cent I liked to achieve. A counterfeiter can never achieve a hundred per cent accuracy of course. The exercise was eventually successful, but it proved to be more of a grounding for a second attempt at them with a different partner a few years later after I had been released from prison. Techniques devised at this earlier stage to overcome the incredible complexities of the photogravure, which are built into the note, only came fully to fruition later on.

The dollar notes from which I made my forgeries were obtained from American Express in London. Did they do nicely? Well, it wasn't possible to get crisp new notes from them but I made sure they were as clean as possible and I touched up on the negatives any marks from the originals likely to spoil my work.

The very first complication in the counterfeiting of the dollar is the nature of the paper itself. If you look at the greenback closely you will notice that unlike sterling it is covered in tiny bits of fibre, blue and red hairs which the naked eye can scarcely detect. They are chucked in by the bucketful when the paper is made and are an essential ingredient of its make-up. It is a primary security device, and it is the first task of the forger, with any pride in his work, to simulate it. With a sharp knife, or pin, you can actually tease the fibres out of the paper until they stick up like frayed pieces of cotton on your whistle. They have a random pattern though, of course, they are added to the paper in fixed quantities by the United States Mint. Although they vary in size a little they're about one sixteenth of an inch long and almost immeasurably narrow.

Their presence did not take me by surprise. I still have some marvellously helpful American text books which, at the time, guided me in my work with information on all kinds of subjects connected with the making of the greenback. Secretive though my own work had to be, I must confess to being a firm supporter of the concept of freedom of information and only wish the British were as open as Uncle Sam.

After trying, and abandoning, the idea of using bits of nylon or wire to simulate the fibres, I solved the problem with frayed fibre from old lengths of electrical flex – you know, the sort used in houses before plastic-covered wiring took over. I scraped and cut up bits of flex over a sheet of paper and then imposed an average count per square inch on my bogus notes. It was not, however, the actual red and blue fibres you could see on my forgeries at the end of the exercise but a photographic impression of them. So mine could not be teased out of the paper, like the real thing, but I knew even the most vigilant cashier would never bother to do that. Just how important the hairs are to the security of the dollar became clear to me when, early on, I returned to American Express in order to exchange for sterling some of the older, genuine greenbacks I didn't need to retain. The chap there immediately put some to the light and accepted them having found the hairs he was looking for. He was not looking for a watermark, for the dollar doesn't have one.

Photographing the fibres was a simple, if tedious, business. I sprinkled them onto plain paper which I had already run through the offset litho to give it the fine lime-green tint with which the greenback is coloured. The camera allowed me the wonderfully useful facility of reducing in size the fibres from the electrical flex, so that I achieved the right diameter and length. My fibres, you see, were slightly bigger than those in the genuine dollar. At the beginning I found I had sprinkled on too much, so I used opaque on the negative to blank out the excess, as well as to reduce the length of some. It was a fiddly chapter in my forging of the dollar but it worked, even though it took six days of printing to get the finished product. My character would not allow me not to bother.

Why did it take six days? The plates I made from the finished negatives had to go through the offset litho six times, each process taking a day, after allowing for drying in-between. The paper first had to go through the machine with the red-coloured hairs on one side, and then the other side; then I changed the ink to blue to repeat the process on both sides for the blue hairs. And all that followed the two days required for applying the lime-green tint to each side. When all had been done, the naked eye could scarcely detect any difference from the way the virgin paper looked before printing, given the lightness of the tint and the minute size of the fibres. It looked just like off-white paper. I remember being pretty pleased with myself, but perhaps a bit forlorn when the glory had worn off that I still had to print everything else which makes a dollar a dollar.

The application of the tint itself provided me with an early indication of how difficult it was going to be to counterfeit the authentic greens of the dollar. I found that, in daylight, I would achieve exactly the right depth of colour and confidently print it. But the following day, when the paper was dry, it was considerably lighter. It was like turning a human being into a damned ghost; the colour just seemed to evaporate. I'd look at it and say to myself: "What's the matter with you? This isn't what I printed yesterday. Where does this come from?" At first I thought I was going colour-blind. The trick was, I discovered after an awful lot of aggravation, to use the ink much darker than seemed right. By the time it had gone through a screen – the plate with all the dots in – and dried, it finally came out right.

The rich variety of green which makes up the dollar also meant that the paper had to be run through the offset litho at a much slower rate than the 20,000 sheets a day of which the machine was capable. I couldn't run at that speed to maintain high-quality registration and convincing colour differentiation. But problems of colour and of simulating paper fibre were almost incidental by comparison with the main task in hand.

Counterfeiting by photo-lithography the superbly engraved dollar is like finding a way through Hampton Court maze on a foggy night, so ingenious is its design. It makes the twenty-pound note and the ten-pound note a piece of cake. If it had not been for my skills as a toolmaker and my infinite patience I'd have torn my hair out at times.

The camera took what seemed a faithful photograph of the note. And it was a damned good camera, too, believe me. But, regardless of the exposure or focus, I found it impossible to capture the whole of the extraordinary variety of fine filigree in one image from which to make the plates. Portions of the original were always missing from my reproduction. One area would reproduce perfectly but another would be like a German soldier at a British prisoner-of-war camp – missing. Equally, another attempt with the camera, using a different exposure, would restore the missing bit to my image but, frustratingly, forfeit something else. Alternatively, I would find I would achieve perfect reproduction of one area of the filigree, but another would be blacked-out like a smudge in a schoolboy's exercise book. The plates which I produced from these negatives were next to useless. I'd keep going back to basics and take a photograph at F8 for ten seconds, say, then another at fifteen seconds, and yet another at twenty seconds. Then I'd make plates of those. Dissatisfied with the results, I would try F22 at ten, fifteen and twenty seconds. And so on. But no matter what I tried, there would still be a bit of this missing, or a bit of that blacked out.

How can I best describe the effect of all these imperfections? Well, the President – I think it was Mr. Jackson on the twenty-dollar bill and Mr. Grant on the fifty, though I've no idea if this reflects American opinion of their respective merits as head of state – had continuous lines engraved on his forehead, no doubt from the cares of office. One of them at least, probably whoever had the louder dress sense, also wore a check coat. A faithful representation of the lines on his face in my forgery, however, inescapably turned the coat into a black garment in which an undertaker would have felt at home (or at work, at any rate). Likewise, a perfectly reproduced cross-lined check coat made the President look years younger than he was meant. Yes, the lines on his face were missing.

Those are examples of just two small areas of the genuine greenback whose reproduction conflicted. I could mention more, as in one of the very earliest samples of the forgery which I took up to Maddox Street for Fred to inspect.

The big man said: "The sky's missing over the White House."

Yes, it was supposed to be cloudy; whereas lines were engraved on the original there was none on mine.

Ominously, Fred added: "You'll have to do better, Charles."

To overcome the problem I adapted the technique I had earlier devised for excising my signature from the traveller's cheques, the only difference being that I employed it several times over on the same note. It was a bit like building a police photofit picture from several parts and, in another sense, like a collage. I photographed the same note in the same position several times over, varying exposure and focus as needs required, and punched the negatives for perfect registration. Then, I took the best parts from each, ensuring that every single area of the note was properly reproduced on at least one negative. Finally, I sat down with a light box and an eyeglass and masked out with opaque all the useless or poor parts on the negatives. On the plate I stuck the pinbar register; the edited negatives I mounted on that and made an exposure. So I might, for example, have a negative with no face – just the lines of the forehead.

It didn't matter how little was on a particular negative, so long as what was left after editing it was of high quality. Building up the picture this way was a task guaranteed to send most people on a Cresta run to lunacy. But patience is one of my virtues and the finished article was absolutely fantastic. No other counterfeiter had ever used the technique before. All my rivals reviewed their negatives and simply chose the best one, regardless of imperfections. Their best might have been only seventy-five per cent good and to me that does not set a high enough standard. Theirs fooled most of the people, most of the time, but by the time I had perfected my own technique, the forged greenback deceived bank experts.

It was during the forging of the dollar that I really came to understand the complexities of colour and how to use ink correctly. A kid will tell you the primary colours are red, yellow, green and blue – though the red is more of a purple and the blue more of a blue-green – and to these white and black may be added. It still amazes me that from just this handful, any colour you care to name is derived. Of the 100 or so different hues which have been detected in the spectrum, only these few contain no suggestion of another hue. Take a look at any imaginative half-tone picture in a posh colour magazine – light gleaming on a bottle of champagne, the shadow of a tree upon water – and the dots of colour before your eyes are actually derived from the four printing primaries of black, yellow, blue and red.

The controls available to me in getting a colour right included mixing, diluting with white, darkening with black, and, from a simple technical point, a handy ratchet by the ink-duct on the offset litho to govern the amount of ink I used. But the key to understanding half-tone colours is to remember that by printing in tiny dots on paper, you are effectively mixing your ink with the colour of the paper. That is why, when you are printing on white paper, the ink always has to be darker than you would imagine proper. Ink, too, always dries lighter than it goes on. Another useful tip to remember in order to maintain constancy of colour is to buy ink from one manufacturer alone, no matter which one, and stick with him. It is asking for trouble to buy ink from more than one because of variations in shade. I used to buy a set of about ten colours at a time from which I could make up all the hues of the rainbow.

One aspect of counterfeiting which I did not master at this stage of my career, though I was determined to do so, was the choice of paper. It was after I came out of prison that, like the lady in the advertisement who discovered a particular brand of vodka, I discovered Optimum 80. It was principally useful to the legal profession for documents like wills and contracts which were meant to last, and I'm quite sure the manufacturers never realised how helpful it would be to Charles Black in his forger's den. It had one hundred per cent rag quality which meant it was non-fluorescent under ultra-violet light, was naturally non-absorbent, and was similar in feel to the actual dollar bill, after I had given it the special Charles Black treatment. Furthermore it had the kind of foldability which any high spender with a much used wad of notes in his back pocket naturally expects if his money is not to fall to pieces.

Although the paper I used while forging dollars for Fred served its purpose it did not compare to the Optimum 80 in strength and flexibility. Moreover, without my realising it at the time, it constantly threatened to give the game away. That was because, as a bonded paper made from woodpulp instead of rags, and treated with size and china clay to make it non-absorbent, it was incriminatingly fluorescent under ultra-violet light. Real dollar bills, you see, are not supposed to be luminous like the shirt cuffs of the Black and White Minstrels. My earliest forgeries were, I'm afraid, though you would not have known it unless you had taken one out of your wallet at a psychedelic discothèque for it to be bombarded by a revealing stream of radiation from the ultra-violet lighting.

The inferior paper which I used at this stage had a further drawback – the manufacturer's watermark. It does not require a genius to understand that the watermark-free dollar would look less than convincing if it were to bear the imprint of Fred Bloggs & Co, paper-makers of East London, on my otherwise faithful reproductions. I eradicated the unwanted watermark in a rather amateurish way, there being no obvious alternative. After printing three or four bills on each sheet of A4 paper and guillotining them, I checked each under the light and threw out those which bore the offending mark.

When a counterfeiter is in full production, printing thousands of notes, errors will easily creep in without the greatest vigilance. I'm thinking not just of greenbacks with the paper-manufacturer's watermark, greenbacks without the White House sky and greenbacks without the lines in the President's forehead – but greenbacks, for instance, where the number at the top of the note doesn't match the number at the bottom. Attempting to pass forgeries with such an elementary imperfection as this, seems to me the height of folly; they are fit only for burning. Mind you, customers can be strange animals.

I remember Fred telephoning me one day from Maddox Street while I was in the dark-room working on some Post Office Giros, to ask if I had disposed of a pile of notes which I regarded as unfit for general circulation. It so happened that at the time I had a pile of several thousand bills of different denominations awaiting the right wind for me to light a bonfire. I asked Fred why he wanted to know.

"I think, dear boy, I can sell them," he said, not a little jubilantly. "Special discount of course."

"You can't possibly sell them, they're rubbish," I said. "I've got a reputation to maintain."

"Listen Charlie, did you hear me? I said I can sell them. Bring them up to me."

So, anxious not to offend the big man, I reluctantly took off for Maddox Street with many a glance over my shoulder, carrying a large brown-paper parcel containing over 3,000 notes of poor quality counterfeit currency.

Fred said: "We can get two pounds each for these."

This was only a fraction of what we normally charged but it was like trading old rope for good money and Fred was never one to look a gift-horse in the mouth. At this stage I didn't know who was the customer, and never asked, but he paid up and I thought no more about the deal. But it's a small world, isn't it? Later on I heard that a prisoner I'd become friendly with the first time I was banged up was indirectly involved in a sequence of events which led to the arrest of Fred's aforementioned customer. This is what happened.

My prison acquaintance had a girlfriend whose father was a bookmaker (amazing how often that profession crops up in the annals of the criminal fraternity, isn't it?). Well, the poor man got shot one day for a reason unknown to me. The police, no doubt acting on good intelligence, raided a number of clubs. In one of them at least they searched everybody with two legs. And, as Lady Luck would have it, one of the people in there, minding his own business, was Fred's unfortunate customer. His pockets, of course, were overflowing with my imperfect dollar bills, though why he should have taken them into the club I don't know. So it was goodnight to him.

Two important procedures completed the task of making my counterfeit dollars. The first of them, numbering the notes, can be a veritable poacher's trap for the unwary forger who decides to print his own numbers without understanding what he is doing. The numbers, like the medallion or seal, are in bright green on the front of the note which is otherwise printed in black. Merely copying the same number as the original as part of the overall process of counterfeiting – as I did in my earliest batches – is obviously considerably easier than printing your own numbers onto the forgery afterwards. But equally obviously such an approach means that you need luck on your side if you, or a customer, then pass more than one note at a time of the same number. Numbering your own notes is thus a nuisance but, as far as I am concerned, a worthwhile chore whether it be by hand or by letterpress. The catch is you have to understand the American numbering system.

From reading educative official American books and pamphlets I discovered that the numbers only go up to L – the twelfth letter of the alphabet. Each letter corresponds only to the name of the bank on the seal or medallion on the front. And the number which follows the initial A to L letter is correspondingly fixed up the numerical scale to 12. I was awfully grateful to make the discovery; after all, printing notes with a M to Z prefix on the seal might land one in hot water.

As I write, I am looking at a Federal Bank of Dallas one-dollar bill, a genuine one which just happens to be in my possession. The letter K is the first character in the bank identification number, and it is printed on the front four times, beside the number eleven. So it would be a foolish forger who ignored the formula or printed the K eleven on a Bank of Wisconsin bill. Understanding plate, series and issue numbers is vitally important if you don't want to be rumbled.

The numbering complete, I was particularly proud of the final treatment I gave my dollar bills after they had come off the offset litho. It was a kind of icing on the cake, though I must confess I borrowed the idea from an Australian counterfeiter I'd heard about. Original though my approach to forgery was, I was never too proud to incorporate the proven technique of others. To give the notes that special silkiness which makes their feel a vitally important component, I dipped them in glycerine which I bought in small bottles from the chemist. Although this messy stuff is insoluble I mixed it with water in a bucket and thrashed it around for a while to produce small globules. Then I soaked the notes in it for about ten minutes. I tried putting them in the wife's tumble-drier afterwards but when that didn't achieve the right results, I dried them over fan heaters.

They came out with a slight curl which no amount of pressing would eradicate completely and so they had the appearance of used notes – no bad thing really for the sake of verisimilitude, especially as I'd found it impossible to acquire new dollar bills in England. The only disadvantage was that they could not then be passed in numerical sequence for obvious reasons.

In each process of dollar production I sought perfection and was only able to attain it after I had recommenced work following my release from prison. Curiously though I found in some respects that the American Mint itself permitted production variations in its glorious greenback, if not imperfections. Sometimes I found that the genuine article was not perfectly centred on the paper, sometimes there would even be the slightest variations in the size of the note itself, and sometimes the background lime-green tint would be a little yellower, or whiter, than others I took to be normal. I decided the most sensible response to all this was to produce my forgeries to a perfect medium, printing dead centre, and in colours whose variation was undetectable.

Undetected was what I too remained for the three profitable months I was in dollar production – until a little bit of earlier villainy caught up with me.

6

I knew the cops were waiting for me the moment I turned the corner into Garden Road after dropping the children at school. The police-car, waiting outside the Black residence, was unmarked but I can smell such a vehicle a mile off. I suppose I could have driven on, but I had nowhere else to go, and the role of a runaway from the law wouldn't suit me. I've always much preferred to talk my way out of trouble; besides, I wouldn't know how to pitch a tent if I chose to vanish into Epping Forest.

It was a pleasant September morning – far too pleasant to be arrested on – and I had the window of the car wound down. This was just as well, because half-way along the short distance between the corner of the road, and my house, I spotted a familiar figure heading for number twenty-eight. It was my new part-time partner, the light-fingered acquaintance from the firm of security printers, and he was on his way to work at my place. No doubt he was thinking, as I had been on the drive back from school, about another profitable day's employment in the dark-room churning out greenbacks. Stanley would be on duty in the shed that day but there was at that moment no sign of him.

In the best American B-movie tradition I slowed the car down when I was parallel to my partner and slipped him a message out of the corner of my mouth without turning my head.

"Keep walking, I think we've got visitors."

The fellow cottoned on in an instant, and kept going in the direction of Sundridge Park Golf Course, looking to all intents and purposes as if he hadn't a care in the world. I wished I could have joined him because the moment I pulled into my driveway, I knew the game was up. Four plain-clothes officers jumped me and produced a warrant to search the house.

It wasn't my life which flashed before me as it's supposed to do in these circumstances, just the past few months. I could see all my hard work going up in smoke. What I couldn't figure out was how they'd come to point the finger at me when I'd been such a cautious counterfeiter. The officers invited me in to my own home and I knew there was absolutely nothing I could do to prevent them finding everything – negatives, plates, printing press and all, cosily in place in a suburban counterfeiter's den in full production of the US dollar.

Once inside the front door, one of the officers asked me: "What have you been up to then, Charlie?"

Naturally I replied: "What's all this about?"

The same man went on: "Don't come the old innocent with me. We have information that you used forged instruments to obtain goods."

It was a classic example of police-speak, but actually the words were specially illuminating.

"Well, I know nothing about it," I replied, realising in a flash that the visit had nothing to do with my counterfeiting business. A time-bomb had unexpectedly blown up in my face and the fuse had been six months burning. It was back in the spring, you will recall, when I was strapped for cash while researching how to build a forger's den and print my own money, when I travelled down to the South Coast with some stolen banker's drafts and robbed a number of jewellers of some of their finest items. After all this time I'd assumed I'd got away with it and scarcely gave the matter a thought.

But sleeping dogs have a habit of waking up and barking. It transpired that my South Coast accomplice, Ben, who had as many previous convictions as there are diamonds at the Ritz, had blown the whistle on me. Thus it was that three of my visitors, perfect gentlemen all, were actually from Bournemouth police; the other officer was a detective inspector from the local nick but he, believe me, was a little less charming. I know that in my line of business one has to be circumspect about the way police choose to conduct themselves. So I'm not complaining when I tell you this one was of the type who doesn't mind the use of physical persuasion when he wants you to help with his inquiries. Fortunately, though, my inquisitor, who had accompanied the others in a liaison capacity, soon had to zoom off on another matter – auditioning for a part in a horror movie, I shouldn't wonder. His departure was just as well because he was a wide-awake copper and he wouldn't have missed a trick, I'm sure, which is more than might be said for his three country colleagues.

I had experienced a moment's relief upon discovering that the raid had nothing to do with my counterfeiting operation, but my heart quickly returned to my boots when I realised it was inevitable that the remaining three officers would soon uncover rather more than they had bargained for when they set off from Bournemouth. Curiously it was my boots, or more precisely a pair of black shoes, together with a striped black suit which I had worn that day on the coast which these detectives began looking for. They were part of the description of me given to police by the aggrieved jewellers.

But before the search, which was to last an agonising seven hours, really got underway, my friend Stanley was to play a cameo role in the drama. Unbeknown to me Stanley had arrived for work before my return from dropping the kids off at school and was ensconced in the shed. Frankly I'd forgotten all about him. From where he was he could not have spotted that I had company in the house, the shed being secure from prying eyes inside as well as out. The assembled throng in the kitchen suddenly had its first sighting of my diminutive partner in crime through the window as Stanley emerged. Maybe it was his acting experience at the police station when he reported his car missing which helped him master the situation. Without showing it, Stanley clocked the fact that a surprise party was in full swing in the kitchen. As cool as you like he turned to lock the shed door before ambling past the right-hand side of the kitchen and disappearing down the side alley.

"Who's that?" asked one of the detectives.

"Oh, he's only an odd-job man – does a bit of gardening for me," I said, before quickly adding "hasn't actually started on the garden yet." (The weeds stretched in every direction as far as the eye could see.)

Stanley, whose car I hadn't actually noticed upon arrival from school, casually got into the vehicle and drove off. It was just as well that from the back of the house where we had congregated the police were not to know that my alleged handyman was the owner of a 3.8 S-type Jaguar. With alarm bells ringing in his head my partner scarcely drew breath until he reached Maddox Street where he alerted the others, I later discovered. It was only after this had been accomplished that Stanley permitted his nervous breakdown to begin.

Once the local Detective Inspector had gone the remaining officers began their search and quickly found the shoes and suit they believed I had worn on the day of the crime. After making an initial overall inspection they then began to comb the house, though I wouldn't swear they knew what they were looking for. I assume it must have been some more stolen banker's drafts to link me more positively with the crime in question, at least that's what I'd have searched for if I'd been them.

In the hall was a cupboard which was bursting at the seams with literature on machine tools and engineering in general. That engaged the three officers for a long time. In the master bedroom I had a filing cabinet and a desk. In fact it was more like an office, as my wife would testify. The filing cabinet was full of all kinds of bits and pieces but principally the discarded fruits of some of my smaller inventions. These kept them well occupied. Then they climbed into the loft where I had a lifetime's collection of personal papers and other bumph of every description. That lot tied them up a while.

They took hours going from bedroom to bedroom, living-room to kitchen, boiler-room to garage, painstakingly examining every little thing. After the initial shock had worn off and I had resigned myself to my fate I turned my thoughts to my talkative friend Ben who had dropped me in it. He was a fraudster of long standing and he wanted me to join him in some enterprise which would have involved my flying to Hong Kong to set up an office. As I saw it in the circumstances a very slow boat to China seemed rather more appropriate.

At some stage or other in mid-afternoon one of the officers emerged from the boiler-room looking not unlike a Black and White Minstrel after inspecting a worthy collection of pots and pans of doubtful value to anyone but a rag-and-bone man. The good man came in for a wash and brush-up and he was not amused. But the interesting thing about him was that he seemed to have lost his taste for the search. And by that time his two colleagues were enjoying tea and biscuits which my wife set out for them in the kitchen. (I wished she had served their refreshment in the lounge because right outside the kitchen was my overwhelmingly large garden shed; you just could not look out of the window and miss it.) Nevertheless, with the passage of time and evidence that the officers were flagging, I began to feel just a little bit chirpier than I had all day. I knew the three detectives wanted to return my hospitality by taking me back to Bournemouth with them for an identification parade. Given that they had already driven up to London early that morning I suspected that they might just be getting in the mood to go home to their wives or girlfriends.

My wife was, of course, bemused by the whole drama though I suppose she knew me well enough not to do something silly such as ask me in the presence of our visitors what on earth was going on. While I was sitting alone with her in the kitchen I managed to say: "I hope they don't go looking in certain places." She still imagined I was printing soft pornography, of which she preferred never to speak. Joan shrugged her shoulders and replied: "I expect they'll find it sooner or later – whatever it is."

But they didn't. It was a classic oversight for which I cannot account to this day, quite incomprehensible. Maybe they were psychologically satisfied with finding me, my shoes and my suit, but who is to say? As they entered through the front door the open-planned living area of my large house was straight ahead. To the right was a corridor with three doors, one leading to a cupboard and another to a downstairs toilet, both of which they inspected. But the third door, the furthest of them, led to the dark-room, the seat of my forger's den. It was locked but I could scarcely have denied them a key if they had asked for it. They just did not seem to notice its very existence. For seven nerve-racking hours it was as if the room had become invisible. I shudder to think of the promotion these worthy officers missed.

At 4.30pm, with the kids due home from school at any minute and my wife worrying about them finding me in the arms of the law, came the memorable climax to the visit: "Right, we've got the suit and shoes. Let's go." So relieved was I by the outcome of their inquiries I didn't even ask them for a receipt. Like a child waiting to start a trip to the seaside I couldn't wait to get into the police-car and drive down to Bournemouth. I sat in the back seat, having engineered our means of departure from the house so we left via the side alley and not the front where we would have had to pass the dark-room. But there was a final hiccup; there always is.

"Hold on a minute," said one of the officers. "I promised to tell your wife the phone number of the nick."

I said: "Oh, it doesn't matter about that. Let's go."

"No, no, I promised."

"She doesn't care about that."

The officer got out of the car, walked down the drive-way, turned left and went straight past the dark-room where the windows were shielded by Venetian blinds – the third and outer layer of coverings protecting my den from prying eyes – to the front door. His absence sent my old ticker rate up a bit for the several minutes he was away. When he returned I thought he was bound to say "What's that room there, I don't remember it?" But no, not a word. I doubt whether anyone has ever been so relieved as I to be arrested and carted off in a police-car to a certain term of imprisonment. Perhaps my den had become so precious to me I was prepared to serve time for it.

I'm pleased to disclose that, shed and dark-room apart, I left behind one more secret as I watched South London disappear behind me. It was one which the team of detectives could be forgiven for missing; they wouldn't have found it if they'd stripped off the wallpaper. Unknown to my partners I had secretly shot an extra series of negatives of dollar bills of various denominations and punched them to ensure proper registration. I regarded this extra-curricular activity as an insurance policy against an uncertain future. I had such a cracking good camera and I knew the day might come when I got screwed by the fickle finger of fate and lost my equipment. Having the negatives, all of them ready for conversion into half-tone plates, meant I was half-way through the process of counterfeiting a new series if ever the need arose. I wrapped the negatives in brown paper and looked for a hiding-place.

I selected the kitchen door, took it off its hinges, drilled out the bottom so it left a neat hollow inside and, after inserting the package, screwed on a metal plate so nothing would drop out. There my negatives remained, quite happily, for a long, long while. When I eventually came out of prison and resumed my professional activities they afforded me an invaluable beginning.

At Bournemouth police-station I was escorted to the cells and there left to stew for the best part of five days before I was properly interviewed. All the niceties – legal representation, habeas-corpus, that sort of thing – went out of the window but I accepted my circumstances like a well-drilled soldier and certainly didn't complain. I was downstairs in the dungeons and the room-service was zero-star. Banging on the door was pointless because no one ever came, except to deliver food which Oliver Twist would have found inedible. The cell reeked of urine, the only light came through a fanlight, and the only light bulb was dead, so most of the time it was pitch black. To hell with it, I thought. Things might be bad but they could have been a lot worse if I'd been detained as a currency forger instead of a humble passer of stolen banker's drafts.

I have been blessed with a high tolerance of most things unpleasant and an ability to go into suspended animation. So I slept most of the time and, in waking periods, relished my good fortune. If you discipline yourself then the worst hardship is normally bearable. Much as I prefer my freedom, I've always been able to adapt to incarceration. So five days went by. Then all of a sudden the door was opened by a detective inspector and the torture was over.

"Hello, Charlie, how are you?" he asked, doubtlessly expecting me to cry for mercy.

"Terrific, thank you," I replied. "I think I must have been working too hard and this was just the sort of rest I needed. How are you?"

106

"I've got a few questions to ask you," he said, a bit crestfallen. "We've been trying our best to arrange an identity parade for you but it's been a bit of a job – you know, trying to get all the witnesses here at the same time. That's why you've been kept hanging around. You sure you're all right?"

My friends, the jewellers from Brighton, Worthing and Bournemouth, whom I hadn't had the pleasure of seeing for six months, duly arrived the next day when they unerringly picked me out of the parade. Meanwhile I refused to answer any of the Detective Inspector's questions, or to sign anything. Never do that because it will only get you into deeper water. I've heard it said that if you're accused of stealing an apple just deny it without elaboration. Never say you didn't do it because you don't like apples anyway. A prosecution witness will only turn up in court to testify that Granny Smith is your favourite relative, and her apple-pies irresistible to you.

At the local magistrates court, where I faced a charge of obtaining jewellery by putting my moniker to the stolen banker's drafts, I was remanded in custody to Dorchester Prison. It took seven weeks before I got bail. In the meantime I had an interesting visit in Dorchester from my missus and from Fred who explained what had happened after I was driven away by the police.

Stanley's journey, from my shed in Bromley to Soho, which was about as agitated as the messenger's from Ghent to Aix, brought pandemonium to Maddox Street. Everyone there assumed, not unreasonably, that my house had become the centre of the universe for the Yard's counterfeit currency squad and that a manhunt for my accomplices was about to be launched. Would I be forced to give them all away? It was decided after an anguished discussion which lasted all day that the only way to find out was by telephoning Joan to see if she or the police answered. The man deputed to do the job was Stanley. The time was about six o'clock in the evening, about eight hours after he had arrived in Soho to break the news.

"Hello, Joan?" he asked. "Hope I'm not inconveniencing you. Anyone there with you?"

"No."

"Everything all right, then?"

"They've taken Charlie away."

"Yes. Sorry to hear about that. I thought that was what was happening but I didn't want to get in the way." (Long pause) "Did they go into anywhere? You know. Did they go into the front room? Or the shed?"

"No."

"Are you sure?"

"Yes."

"Is anybody standing there with you?"

"No."

"Did Charlie say anything."

"No. What do you mean?"

"You know, about us, me?"

"No."

"I'll phone you back later."

The telephone went dead and another long case conference was convened in Maddox Street in which Stanley was the principal witness.

"This can't be right," said Fred. "I don't believe it. The cops are all there waiting for us to turn up. Well, waiting for you to turn up, Stanley. It's only common sense."

A while later poor Stanley was back on the blower to Joan, with Fred breathing down his neck. The answers were much the same as my long-suffering wife gave the first time.

"They searched the place?"

"Yes, Stanley, I'm still clearing up the mess. If you want to come round and help, you can."

"And they never found . . . never went into the shed or tried the door of the dark-room?"

"No."

Jubilation gradually dried the sweaty palms in Maddox Street and in a matter of days Stanley felt brave enough to return to work in Garden Road. It was good therapy for the little fellow. Big Fred told me to worry about absolutely nothing and after he and the missus had gone I returned to my hibernation in Dorchester.

It was nice spending a family Christmas at home (on bail) especially as I realised that the following year I should almost certainly be doing porridge, instead of turkey and mince pies, for my misdemeanours. But time's winged chariot was ever near. With my trial at Dorchester Crown Court set for two or three months hence I was short of it to put my affairs on a sound financial footing. So I wasted no time in putting my nose to the grindstone to make as much money, forged and real, as possible.

To give him credit, Stanley had done a good job in my absence and we had plenty of work meeting further orders from Fred for dollar bills. I also cracked the problem of making a numbering box and completed the artwork on Postal Orders and Giros so that my partner could print them while I enjoyed the hospitality of life in prison.

One of our best customers for the greenback was a titled man whom good breeding prevents me from naming, with a penchant for gambling in the casinos of Nice and Monte Carlo. Fred knew this gentleman as a reliable spender at the boss's gambling club in London and was happy to supply him with my products. My dollars brought him a lot of success among the high rollers of the Riviera, I'm pleased to say, and he kept coming back for more.

One major coup, however, just slipped our grasp. I don't know how, and was too polite to ask, Fred made this particular contact – a banker in Zurich – but the boss always did mix with some wonderfully influential people. The Swiss gnome in question had been called in to run I don't know which bank, as a temporary measure, after the actual manager suffered a heart attack. In the vaults our friend discovered large reserves of United States dollars and identified an excellent opportunity to make himself even richer than he was already. The plan was for us to supply him with millions of dollars which he was going to switch with the real ones. He felt that in the unlikely event of the switch being uncovered later by the auditors he would hardly be suspected in view of his brief tenure of the job. But the deal never went through. I'm uncertain why the sting never got beyond the planning application. But I think the gnome wanted a much bigger discount than Fred was prepared to countenance. Or it may have been that the man simply lost his bottle.

Nevertheless the dollars I printed allowed me to maintain a good income while I was awaiting trial, and the Postal Orders and Giros promised more as I budgeted for bleaker times ahead. But the crowning glory of my few months at liberty was much more exciting than all this put together. The time had come I decided to remind myself that I was an Englishman and turn my attention to the five-pound note, a new series of which had been issued by the Bank of England.

I regarded the challenge merely as a subject of experimentation in the difficult circumstances which prevailed and did not, for instance, bother with finer points such as acquiring the ideal paper on which to print the fiver. But in no time the results were astonishingly good. I only forged a few of them, perhaps a couple of hundred, but the quality actually allowed them to be sold. This was despite an absence of marketing by Fred. My fivers sold for two pounds each and customers kept coming back to ask for more, offering more than half the face value by the time I was forced to retire hurt from the game. It was a dreadfully frustrating business to have to stop after making such a breakthrough.

My well-tried formula of counterfeiting by photo-lithography – you remember, taking negatives through filters to separate the colours and making half-tone plates through screens from these – worked a treat. But then there was no reason why it should not. The blue plate was obviously as heavily employed for the fiver as the green had been for the dollar.

The principal difference between the two currencies, as I'm sure you are anxious to point out, is that unlike the greenback the fiver has a watermark – a design impressed in the manufacture of paper visible only when it is held to the light – and a metal strip to boot. Now, it is always assumed that these distinctive characteristics, the watermark especially, represent the thorniest obstacles to their artificial reproduction, and to some forgers they are insuperable. But that is not the case if you use the Charles Black method of forgery.

The very first task in counterfeiting the five-pound note is to reproduce the metal strip and at first, I must confess, I made the mistake of deviating from photo-lithography. Experiments with strips of aluminium cooking-foil glued between two sheets of paper quickly proved a waste of time, not least because the subsequent printing of the double-thickness forgery did not have the feel, or look, of a Harold Wilson pound in your pocket. I thus turned to a more inventive method which did not compromise my established technique.

On virgin paper I drew a straight line in black ink, the thickness of the metal strip. This I then photographed and printed as a solid line on the otherwise blank A4 paper on which I would be forging the actual notes. The line ran, if I remember correctly, just to the left of where the Queen's nose would be. The next stage was to run the paper a second time through the machine, blanking out, not just the line, but the entire sheet with specially diluted white, opaque ink. In this way the line was rendered invisible until held to the light.

111

Try experimenting yourself by blotting out with diluted deletion fluid a black line you have drawn on a piece of paper and you'll see what I mean. If you can't be bothered just think of a typing error which you have blotted out with white. You can't see the mistake but when you hold the paper to the light you will still find a clear impression of the error.

In one sense the line with which I was left was like the fibres I have described in the dollar bill. Your eye tells you it's there as a real metal strip but all you're looking at is a photographic image of one. Like the fibres, it cannot be teased out with a pin. But your eyes are deceiving you anyway when you look at the metal strip in a genuine five-pound note. It looks black but if you tease it out a little you will find it is actually silver in colour.

One vital matter had to be dealt with, however, before I applied the opaque ink. That was to leave a "window" in the paper, matching the shape of the watermark, which was free from the opaque. That done, the paper was ready for my master stroke, the creation of the watermark itself.

Look at today's fiver and you will see under the light, to the right of the Duke of Wellington and what I take to be the cannons of Waterloo, his ghostly image. There are two full heads to the note I am looking at as I write though more careful inspection reveals that the watermark is actually a continuous column of heads, like a totem pole, which the Bank of England guillotine has cut at the point of his cravat (top) and his eyes (bottom). What the conscientious forger, using my method, has to do is draw the outline of the totem pole on a piece of paper in a ghostly shade of ink. A light box comes in very useful here to help you see what you are doing. The drawing, of course, needs to be meticulous, and so mine was. I then made a plate of my watermark from a photograph I had taken of it. The next stage was to run through the offset litho the paper on which I had already printed the opaqued image of the metal strip. Pin bar registration allowed me to ensure that the new plate, bearing solely the image of the watermark, slotted the Duke precisely into the "window" I had previously reserved for it. Finally, I cautiously opaqued in the offset litho the actual drawn parts of the watermark to render them invisible except through light. When I looked at my finished watermark I thus saw the opaqued photographic image of the parts I had originally drawn, like the outline, hair, nose, eyes, mouth and clothing, combined with white virgin paper in-between.

It's as simple as that. Although my perfectionist approach forced me to draw the watermark as precisely as it is possible, I have to confess that it probably need not have been. The average person will automatically hold a note to the light to verify the presence of a watermark but not study it closely.

Having done all that I simply had to revert to normal photo-lithographic methods to reproduce the complicated filigree of the note, running the paper through the offset litho to apply the different colours separately with plates I had made from the negatives I had taken. By then all that was plainsailing to me.

People suppose that the watermark and metal strip make the forging of a Bank of England note a much more awesome task than the forging of the dollar. They're quite wrong.

7

I felt the judge's displeasure so keenly during my trial at Dorchester Crown Court in February 1972, I thought he was going to reach for his black cap when the time came for sentencing. I escaped the gallows for passing the stolen banker's drafts but I got banged up for five long years. If I'd been appearing at the Old Bailey I'm sure I'd have got a lot less, probably no more than two years. But these bastions of justice in the sticks don't appreciate villains dropping in from London to do their dirty work, and cannot resist making an example of them when they get half a chance. I felt as sick as the proverbial parrot. The wise offender prepares himself mentally for sentencing, reckoning on something like a sixty-forty chance on going down. When the worst happens he's normally ready for it and the first thing he does is divide the term by three to allow for parole. I wasn't prepared for five years. But suicide is much too dangerous a way out so I swallowed hard and thought of England.

I suppose the fact I pleaded not guilty hadn't helped me. My partner in crime, Ben, must have felt he was going on holiday by comparison when he got his eighteen months. Still, the police did get back most of his share of the diamond rings; they never recovered mine. That was one compensation, I suppose. I appealed against the severity of the sentence but that proved to be a waste of time. Thereafter it was a question of knuckling under while I did my porridge. I finished up at Leyhill about eight months later, having served about six at Dorchester and a short time at Bristol, where I was graded as a model fellow, suitable for open prison.

My incarceration was to prove more reminiscent of an extended stay at a holiday camp, without the red-coats, than doing bird at Alcatraz. Within two months of arrival at this happy institution in the Gloucestershire countryside, I was actually standing alone outside the gates in civvies waiting for a bus to take me to the fair city of Bristol. The Home Office, bless it, had agreed to allow me to take a course in catering. Although I took the course seriously and passed a City and Guilds with distinction, by the time I left Leyhill there was, naturally, an ulterior motive behind my application to take it. The once a week release afforded me a ticket to a particularly personal kind of freedom. If I'd been a drinker the ticket would have allowed me to enjoy the watering holes of Bristol with impunity. In fact I don't drink or smoke. But there is one pleasure I really cannot manage without when I'm in prison. It is the company of women. How very unnatural it is that men and women should be deprived of each other when they pay their debt to society. I have no doubt that sexual normality would relieve the prison system of much of its unnecessary tension whether it be through mixed prisons or regular association between prisoners and their partners.

With my have-it-away-day pass I was able to enjoy sex like a normal human being, though my adventures were restricted to a once-a-week performance which accorded with the catering-course timetable. Conscious of my needs, a mate of mine from London used to drive along the M4 with a blonde or a brunette sitting prettily in the passenger seat waiting to accommodate me. Come the lunch hour, they would meet me outside the college where I studied. Then my mate would drive me off to sports field or lover's lane and leave me alone with the lady in question. Talk about day release! My wife never knew, of course, but then I did not want to upset her. Women are lovely creatures but they do seem to confuse sexual freedom with the highest notions of real fidelity. So they're generally best kept in the dark.

Such release did wonders too for my culinary training. The college teachers were much pleased with my appetite for the course and before long I felt free to tell one of them, with whom I got on especially well, that my "wife" was unofficially coming up for the day to see me and to ask if he minded my returning a little late from lunch. The obliging fellow was only too pleased to play a part in easing the strain of my captive life and there were occasions when he let me miss the whole afternoon and marked me present and correct on the register. There are kindly people wherever you care to seek them out. Moreover, once the news broke while I was in prison of the police raid on my home in Garden Road, I began to be treated as something of a celebrity. Everyone wanted to know me and some of the women were only too happy to express their delight in my acquaintance by lifting their skirts.

I was not the only prisoner to enjoy female company, of course. But for most of the rest it was sadly a once a year pleasure, notably on the appropriately named Open Day. That was when wives and girlfriends arrived in their Sunday best for a special visit which frequently ended up in the individual cubicles provided for the inmates.

The good behaviour of the prisoners and the relaxed atmosphere meant that only two or three night-watchmen were left behind on duty in the small hours, and they made checks that all was well only every couple of hours at most. So it was always possible for the more enterprising prisoners to take a break from the rigours of prison life. I never had the need to. But I remember one chap, a local tradesman I think, who enjoyed a breath of fresh air in the night. He used to rise from his bunk and run across the fields to his missus, arriving not too breathlessly I trust to enjoy his conjugal rights. I wouldn't have known but he was in the next cubicle and I used to hear him come and go.

So what is the lesson of all these revelations? It is that the wise prisoner does not buck the system but joins it, in order to manipulate it to his own advantage. And there's nothing new in that; it applies to any walk of life. The man who thinks he will change the world by challenging it is usually a fool or a dead hero.

The day-release system from prison is a fine institution for the best of reasons. It trains people in careers which might never have occurred to them on the outside. So I made sure I took my cooking seriously – well, before lunch at any rate. Then, on Saturday mornings I used to play bowls at a number of civilian clubs in the area around Leyhill. The good burghers must have thought they were doing their bit towards less privileged members of society such as I, and indeed they were, even though playing bowls is not actually my idea of nirvana. Furthermore they fed me. Now such a realistic approach to the art of surviving seems to me considerably more sensible than going bananas and bashing the prison-officers.

Tropical fish are a lot more interesting to me than bowls and the club I established at Leyhill afforded the governor as much pleasure and pride as it did Charles Black. But, more importantly, my interest in the piscine world enabled me to work myself extra rations of freedom, with organised trips out of the prison. An afternoon at the Bristol Zoo aquarium or a morning at a local trout-farm may not sound much of a treat but believe me it's a lot more fun than sewing mail-bags. At first the prison officers didn't relish the concept of escorting a coachful of villains in civilian apparel to the outside world. But when everyone behaved immaculately the screws soon learned what a pleasure such outings could be. We'd be allowed to stop for coffee at a café, or restaurant, after a terrific day out while they'd be spared the rigours of their own working-lives. Sensible enough to let the system work for himself, who could possibly ask for more?

It wasn't exactly in the regulations, of course, but while I was in Bristol I'd get on the blower and telephone the wife; even, on occasions, my business partners. It was actually possible to make appointments for the following week. Life behind bars is what you make it, and the best way to thrive is to show a bit of respect to the officers; to say, "Yes sir, No sir" doesn't hurt and it means you get left alone. It is also advisable to stay clear of the petty crime which goes on and normally involves smoking and drinking. Hootch is made and sold, tobacco is smuggled in for sale. They are the currency of prison life and consequently they are the cause of most disputes.

The one thing which did go wrong for me at Leyhill was the all-important question of parole. Parole is like the sight of an oasis in the desert to every prisoner. After I'd got over the shock of a five-year sentence I automatically divided it by three, and worked out that as a model prisoner I'd be eligible for parole after twenty months. Unhappily my arithmetic led me up the garden path. I didn't bid farewell to Leyhill until September 1974 – a year later than I expected.

Despite my natural good manners and hard labour in the print-shop I was refused the early release I anticipated. I was never told why, but the only possible explanation was the business at Garden Road. You may remember that I exercised my right of those days to refuse to answer questions after the police discovered the forger's den there. The authorities knew they were batting on a sticky wicket when I protested that I could not possibly have had anything to do with it on account of my eighteen month incarceration to date. But they're not stupid and the whole affair at Garden Road obviously put a question mark over me. In the final analysis, the authorities must have concluded that despite the absence of conclusive proof of my involvement they would make me cool my heels for a further year. So, in view of the severity of my original sentence, and the loss of parole, I feel I paid my debt to society for my first venture into counterfeiting. If the buggers don't get you one way they'll make damned sure they get you another way.

Stanley and I never saw each other again after we went our separate ways to prison. I have felt no urge to contact him. Maybe it was the things he said about me during his trial – how I pressured him into joining the operation and how he was terrified of Fred – which damaged the association, but I'm not so sure. Although the allegations were ridiculous I couldn't blame him for saying what he did in order to try to get himself off the hook. The trouble was that his mitigation could not have passed unnoticed by the authorities and must have driven another nail into my coffin with the parole board.

During the eighteen months before the raid on Garden Road, Stanley worked alone. He and our other partner were not terribly fond of each other so they split. It was an arrangement which worked perfectly well because Stanley had become a competent forger after mastering the techniques I taught him, and needed no assistance. But the staff cuts at Garden Road were not the only change in the counterfeiting operation.

Fred, a gentleman when things were going right for him, could be violent when things went wrong – never more so than when he felt threatened. One day things went very wrong indeed. Someone, whose connections shall be nameless, took a fancy to his gambling club and thought it might benefit from the services of a protection agency. Fred took a somewhat different view when the suggestion was made to him. So the man who had the temerity to make it ended up on the floor with a bullet through his head, I'm told, and the body disappeared in a shroud hastily fashioned from the office carpet on which he lay. An awful lot of skulduggery followed including, I later gathered, entirely unworthy suggestions that police-officers were tempted by bribes to cover up the murder.

The upshot of this scandalous affair was that Fred felt obliged to take a long vacation in France while the dust settled. Thus it was that Wheelchair Charlie took over the mantle of management at Maddox Street. The counterfeiting business became a two-man operation with Stanley responsible for the printing and Charlie, the distribution. It was a matter of some months before the police raid on Garden Road that Fred was forced to take refuge abroad. So it really was nonsense for the nervous Stanley to claim in court that he only remained at his post out of fear of what the big man would do to him.

Even with my many varied interests in prison I had plenty of spare time in which to consider my future. I was determined to resume my career in counterfeiting and often dwelt upon ways in which I might improve the merchandise. But, of course, my thinking underwent a rapid reappraisal when I learned that the police had seized the production line. My future depended initially on the set of negatives I had hidden in the kitchen door panel. But, more importantly, I decided I should take a back seat in any future operation, at least so far as the printing of counterfeit currency was concerned. There was no one in the country better than I in setting up an operation and perfecting the artwork; but let someone else take the risk, I thought, in actually rolling the presses.

A number of technical matters kept my mind occupied during the final year of my imprisonment as I contemplated the sort of approach I should adopt. Building myself a smaller camera was an intriguing challenge for starters. Beautiful though the Incaf was, it was unnecessarily large. I began to think small because the smaller things are, the less room they take up, and the less attention they attract. Perhaps with a smaller camera and a smaller plate-maker, which I could also make for myself, I could get away with renting a small office in which to perform all the pre-printing processes. I even considered making my own printing-machine even though I was wary of doing the printing myself again. Table-top printing-machines, which might have suited my purposes, had no register but I toyed with the idea of making and fitting my own. These were some of the thoughts which occupied me as I toiled in the prison print-shop. With the change in circumstances my plans needed to be loose. I knew I had to be patient, once released, and wait for the right opportunity to present itself before I resumed my career. Counterfeiting is such a serious business with such rich rewards that it is foolish to leap into it without proper planning – especially if the police already have your number for a previous excursion into its rarified atmosphere.

My release from Leyhill arrived one fine September day shortly after dawn and I caught the train without delay to London. Reviewing my once thriving forger's den back home was like inspecting the results of a visit from the bailiffs. There was absolutely nothing left of it. Strangely, not even the door to the dark-room remained. I eventually found it leaning against the wall in the shed. That's where the police had left it after taking it off its hinges. A piece had been sawn out of it where the lock had been, presumably so the exhibits officer could produce it at Stanley's trial as proof that he possessed the only key which would fit it. Where the door had been my wife had hung a curtain; carpentry was not her forte.

It was hard to believe from the emptiness of the dark-room and shed that here had been what the press described upon its discovery as the world headquarters of forgery. I wandered aimlessly from one site to the other as if that might resurrect my precious den. But there was no getting away from the fact I'd been wiped out. Even the clock had gone, and the sink for that matter. It was a disturbing experience. Fortunately, however, my lifetime's collection of machine tool equipment – lathes, presses, hacksaw machine, drills etc – remained intact in the garage where I had left it. I came to rely on it after my release for making me a living.

Making small machine tools in my fully equipped garage workshop was second nature to me. Friends of mine, whom I had known in the tool business since my early twenties, came to see me soon after I came out of prison to help put me back to work. I remember doing a lot of work for a firm of scientific instrument makers. Business quickly began to thrive and the wolf disappeared from the door. I found myself quoting for 500 little spindles with threads on, or 1,000 turned pieces with a thread on one end and a square on the other, all kinds of twiddly bits which machines need to engender other machines, metal brackets with holes, and springs which went into holes which went into brackets. You name it, I knew how to make it.

The company used to put orders out to tender and before long I ensured that those I wished to win were awarded to me. I used to telephone a man there, of whom I had made a friend, to ask what was the best quote the company had received for a particular job. At first he protested he wasn't allowed to say. But in the end a combination of charm and expertise won the day. If he'd say two pounds for each item I'd offer to turn it out for a mere one pound ninety-five and send him along a little drink by way of thanks. I got so well known at the firm as the best tool-maker in the business that they used to phone to ask me to put right things made for them by much bigger suppliers than I could even pretend to be. And normally I managed small miracles others would not have bothered to consider.

I had the personal touch, the drive and the inventiveness to make a passably good living. But it was a hassle having to stand all day beside a bench or machine. Making an honest living like that just doesn't seem to suit me for any length of time. The trouble is, it isn't challenging enough, and it doesn't earn enough, regardless of the hours put in. After the rates and the central heating bills have been paid there's never enough left over for the good life. I was chasing my tail to fill my wallet but found there was a limit to what I could expect. Such an existence was too frustrating to continue.

Thankfully by the summer of 1975, without having forged so much as a two-pence piece since my release from prison, the chance of something a little more diverting than machine tool-making finally presented itself. It took me off the straight and narrow, of course, but it gave me the opportunity to live a life more akin to the one to which I had previously grown accustomed. Charles Black became a technical consultant in the counterfeiting business. For the best pay for the least work there's nothing to match the reputation of an expert. You rake it in while other people get their hands dirty.

Two gentlemen, whom discretion prevents me from naming, were introduced to me by an acquaintance from Leyhill. (There's no breeding-ground quite like prison for generating criminal endeavour.) The curious thing about him was that he was serving a sentence for manslaughter. The man had stabbed his wife and earned himself a perfectly reasonable five years, reduced to three on appeal of which he only served one before he got parole. You have to admire the way some people get away with it! Now, his colleagues wanted to buy my expertise for a counterfeiting venture in Crystal Palace. In fact what they wanted me to do was run the whole shooting-match for them but I wasn't prepared to stick my neck out for them. Our agreement was that I should write them out a shopping list, provide all the technical assistance and train them in the finer facets of forgery before withdrawing gracefully with my fee. I didn't want to go near the place once it was in production.

My new colleagues were in the business of forging banker's drafts, having acquired the flavour from some stolen samples of the genuine article. Their plan was to exchange forgeries for Krugerrands, though I didn't know their *modus operandi* and didn't want to. I had to take them on trust because they weren't overloaded with cash and agree to a cut of the proceeds. After they'd done their shopping – some of it from Exchange & Mart – I had to go to their burgeoning den above a shop in Whitehorse Lane to help install the equipment.

The only significant difficulty the two men encountered – apart from the fact they got busted about six months later – was the next-door neighbour, a nosey little creature who wouldn't leave them alone. I thought at the time that the site chosen for the den was less than perfect, though that was none of my business. What I did not realise was that it adjoined the neighbour's bedroom. After he made various inquiries about what my associates were up to, I was forced to fix several layers of acoustic tiles on the partition wall between the two buildings. But I can still picture our curious friend holding an eggcup to his ear against the wallpaper on his side.

Forging banker's drafts was a minor exercise to a man of my experience and the operation proved highly successful. For my time-and-method assistance as a systems analyst I was rewarded with twenty-nine Krugerrands. I cashed them in and bought an apartment in Spain, plus a speed-boat with the small change. Not bad for a part-time consultancy!

The fickle finger of fate intervened when one of my partners, who was wanted for something else, unwittingly led the watching police back to the den one night.

I was once again dabbling in the machine-tool business a little after this episode when interrupted by another proposition. This time a long-firm fraud was involved – if you haven't heard of the term it's to do with a bogus company which builds up a vast quantity of merchandise on tick before disappearing off the face of the earth without the approval of its creditors. The man in charge of the operation had concluded his business but was left with a mountain of Swiss watches which worked less than well, and a pile of metal chains he'd have preferred to be gold. Like Midas, I turned the chains into gold with no difficulty, gold-plating probably hundreds of thousands by dipping them into a heated vat for twenty seconds a time. The poor punters who bought them from a battalion of market-stall wide-boys were convinced of the value of their purchase by a card accompanying each chain which proclaimed it to be nine carat gold. A year or two after buying it, the purchaser would find the gold camouflage wearing thin, revealing a colour which shone less lustrously than rich yellow.

From the mountain of watches I sorted about 150 which needed special attention. They were worth perhaps twenty pounds each. Some I had to cannibalise like a surgeon, others tickle back to life again. It was often tedious work but it paid well for six months or more.

The man who employed me on this production line meanwhile introduced me to a friend who offered me work more in keeping with my forte. He wanted me to set him up with a big hydraulic press at his premises in Sheen Lane, East Sheen. The business temporarily converted me from a paper currency forger into a coin maker. This was a task I relished. As a student of currency I have always been fascinated by the ancient origins of coins. I'm talking of the time when iron rings were used, long before gold, silver and copper coins were first pressed and many centuries before the introduction of paper money.

It never ceased to amaze me how my reputation seemed to precede me at this time; approaches from every likely villain who fancied his chances as a forger were offered.

The hydraulic press, of which I had no experience, was intended to manufacture half-sovereigns. My new partner had the dies, the engraved stamp for striking the coin, but he didn't have much of an idea how to use them. For that matter, neither did I. But, nothing ventured, nothing gained. I soon picked up the subject. The coins were a lot easier to counterfeit than paper money, though not nearly as profitable, of course. This was the next stage of my consultancy period and it was arranged on the same terms as before – expert advice for a good return, but no dirty hands from the business in question. I hadn't long been out of custody and I didn't fancy an early return.

You wouldn't believe the size of the press which arrived one day from somewhere in Dartford. It was tons heavy and must have altered the geology of South London. How do you forge half-sovereigns? Well, you make a blank (in our case from copper, and I shan't tell you where that was obtained because it was none of my business) and, between the die and the vast weight of the press, Bob's your uncle. The blank came out with a perfect image and the proper knurled edge after I tapped it out of the die. The only precaution was to ensure you didn't get your fingers caught.

The only thing wrong with the product at this stage was the metal from which it was made. But I rectified that by dipping it into my faithful pot of gold. The half-sovereigns were destined for insertion in rings – a fashion favoured by a certain type of person with whom it is wise not to exchange blows. Such treatment thus made it impossible to check its weight and discover that all that glistens is not necessarily gold.

That at least describes the plan of action. But before I got to the stage of perfecting a production line my temporary partner got busted. There must be just as high a mortality rate in the coin game as in more lucrative forms of currency counterfeiting. My friend was involved in all kinds of misdemeanours and he actually died while on trial, poor fellow. But he took a police officer or two with him. When he was arrested he started naming names. There were some terrible corruption scandals in those days which would make your hair stand on end. It was a shame the counterfeiting came to nothing. The dies were perfect and the hydraulic press working such a treat that between them they would have turned out coins like an over-generous fruit machine.

Interestingly, the dies which the police of course recovered came from the once fair city of Beirut. It much saddens me how the industrious and innovative Lebanese have let their country go to pot in recent years. Nowadays all that seems to come out of it is cannabis and bloodshed. At the time of which I speak the best die-makers came from Beirut. These people would make anything you cared to ask.

In fact Fred at one time made a fantastic living from sovereigns made in Switzerland from Lebanese dies. He sold them in Hatton Garden to the most reputable of concerns. They were first-class forgeries genuinely made of gold. The trick was that Fred charged the normal buyer's premium – without having paid for it of course. A bit like a VAT fraud, I suppose.

8

It was at the huge annual printing exhibition in London, in September 1975, about twelve months after my release from prison, that the seeds of my second adventure in currency counterfeiting were sewn. The exhibition is a bit like the Boat Show for the printing trade, designed for anyone like me with the smell of ink in his nostrils. It is a wonderful bazaar of cameras, printing-machines, plate-makers, folding-machines, stapling-machines, with dozens of stands for ink makers, paper makers, makers of paste-up tables and, of special interest to me, stands where the Japanese displayed state-of-the-art technology, with inscrutable smiles, which suggested they were taking over the industry just as they have so many others. I found it even more inspiring than I had when I first attended, prior to setting up my den at Garden Road, probably because this time I understood fully what I was looking at.

I remember I was looking at a stand of colour separation machinery from Japan when my attention was diverted by the familiar long blond locks of the man in front of me. They belonged to an acquaintance of mine, Brian Katin, who seemed as mesmerised as I by the equipment on display. I was about to tap him on the shoulder when he turned. Neither of us had to ask the other what he was doing there. The pair of us went off for a cup of tea and, by the time we had concluded a fascinating conversation, a partnership had been formed. It was to prove so technically successful that, police have told me since, the currency we forged made the hairs stand up on the necks of treasury officials.

My friend, a man about twenty years younger than I, explained that while I was in prison he had moved from North London to Pagham on the Sussex coast. A firm of printers for whom he had worked had closed down. His redundancy money had helped him buy a bungalow; more intriguingly it had also helped buy him an offset litho printing-machine. This handsome little number he kept in a secret room at the back of his garage.

The real art of counterfeiting was out of his frame but he had learned enough to believe he could launch himself into business. A jobbing printer in Bognor Regis with both letterpress and offset litho facilities provided Brian with some local work and this helped broaden his knowledge of the trade.

I learned over our cup of tea that, despite all this, Brian's private business was not proving as successful as he had expected. He had been trying to forge dollar bills but the results, he confessed, were little short of abysmal. Photography and plate-making remained much of a mystery to him, and he was actually on the point of throwing in the towel, when the wheel of fortune turned and threw us together. Without needing any persuasion I accepted his invitation and within days drove down to Pagham to inspect his premises.

I got on quite well with the man despite the one weakness in his personality – he always suspected a plot was being hatched against him and his sometimes obsessional suspicions even extended to me. It used to annoy me that Brian always counted his money when we received our payments. There is such a thing as honour among thieves and I resented his lack of trust. In the end, tired of Brian querying whether he was getting his fair share of the profits, I told him to go and find his own outlets.

At the exhibition, I felt no serious doubts that the two of us could work together.

I felt ready to resume my career and needed the

partnership, but, upon inspecting his forgeries at Pagham, decided that he needed me rather more badly. I've seen more realistic currency on a Monopoly board, a sad fact which screwed up the man with frustration. He clearly knew little or nothing about photography, about plate-making or about using the right paper. Without my expertise he was finished.

What an estate agent would have made of his premises I cannot imagine, but to me the bungalow was a desirable residence of the first order. Right across the detached garage, Brian had built a solid wall behind which was a light-proofed forger's den containing a tempting array of equipment which the poor man did not know how to use. It was approached by a secret door. As a camouflage he had packed the front part of the garage with the kind of junk which people who don't worship their cars normally cram in – lawnmowers, oil cans, deckchairs, that sort of stuff. You couldn't move in there, let alone park a car.

My part of the deal was to provide the exquisite set of dollar negatives which I had long ago stashed away inside the kitchen door, or rather plates which I still had to make from them. With this, and my skills, he was, believe me, getting a bargain. Having to supply the paper and a guillotine was also down to me. For my part this was an excellent arrangement. It meant I could leave the incriminating business of printing the dollars entirely to him, sixty-five miles away from Garden Road and the long arm of the law. Of course I had to make a plate-maker and perform all the artwork in order to fulfil my end of the deal, but that I knew I could do with comparative ease at home.

It was just as well that my set of negatives obviated the need for photographic equipment – so long as we remained happy to concentrate entirely on forging dollars. You see Brian's camera was not awfully impressive. The man had bought a cheap and cheerful one for about

£600 when, for forging purposes, he needed an outlay approaching £3,000 even in those days. Small wonder that the so-called artwork on his forgeries would not have fooled a donkey with cataracts. On the kind of camera necessary for our work there is a vacuum pump which sucks the air out to ensure the film lies absolutely flat when you shoot a picture; his one had a pumping device which seemed to me more suitable for sweeping the carpet. You get what you pay for in this world, and Brian hadn't paid enough.

My partner did, however, have a jolly good, substantial offset litho printing machine – better than the one I had had at Garden Road – parked in his secret den. The only trouble was it didn't work properly. The firm which reconditioned and sold it to him had it wrongly assembled. It was alright for messing about with but it refused to pick up when it was meant to produce a print-run. This meant I would have to get my hands dirty stripping it down and rebuilding it. But first I paid a visit to the firm in London, from which it had come, to seek a little technical advice in order to diagnose the problem. By prevaricating when an over-helpful technician there offered to drive to Pagham to examine the machine, I persuaded him instead to take me through the mechanics on another model at his premises. Thus I established the fault on Brian's; it was simply a cylinder lever which had been secured the wrong way round. Unhappily, however, the only way to get at it was by taking the whole machine to pieces.

I'm rarely happier than when surrounded by the cogs and wheels of a mechanical problem so the two days and nights I then spent at Pagham rebuilding the offset litho were both challenging and rewarding. By the time I had finished it worked beautifully.

Back at Garden Road the time had come to indulge in a spot of improvisation in order to produce the plates from the dollar negatives. Plates and plate-makers are not the fancy pieces you might suspect in the counterfeiter's armoury. I used the base of an old plate-maker which I had previously discarded to make a new one, and built a light unit of fluorescent tubes to go on top. This left me with an efficient, reliable one about two foot square by six inches high which I could easily hide under the bed if necessary and which only an expert could identify for what it was. Next I bought chemicals and boxes of virgin plates, which are about the thickness of thin cardboard and cost one pound a go. Security did not seem to me a major difficulty, as long as I got the completed plates out of the house and down to Pagham, as soon as I had got them ready. And I needed little accommodation to do the job, choosing to work in a small dressing-room next to the main bedroom.

Plates vary in size according to the printing-machine for which they are intended, and are pin-bar punched to fit over two claw-like arrangements which hold them in place round the cylinder. The plate has a surface which is sensitive on one side only to ultra-violet light. You put your negative against the sensitive side and expose it to the plate by applying the light source. The image is thus transposed, leaving you with something like a metal negative after it has been developed – a process for which I chose to use the bath (normally when the missus wasn't in the house!).

Before making the plates, however, I had a huge amount of hard work to perform with an eyeglass on the negatives. Using opaque and red transparent tape I went through the business I have already described of taking the best and blanking out the worst details of each negative – of making sure the President's head and coat were perfectly reproduced despite the conflicting focus. Whereas it takes no more than three minutes to expose a normal image on a plate, it would take perhaps twenty-five minutes to build a collage with which I was satisfied. But it was rewarding work for it left me with a perfect image of the greenback from which Brian could print.

Eventually I emerged from the bedroom with plates for twenty, fifty and one hundred dollar bills which I delivered to Pagham. Before Brian printed them we had weeks of messing about getting the colours right. The system we later fixed on, however, was that having perfected the colour we used an ink-maker to make it up for us, supplying maybe ten cans at a time. Both Brian and I were perfectionists and it was at least eight months before we actually got into production. But before that happened I had an uninvited visit from the boys in blue at Garden Road which nearly brought the whole venture to a premature end.

I had just returned from a pleasant trip to Spain and was left with some traveller's cheques, genuine ones, which I wanted to cash in. So I took myself off to Charing Cross, where I had some business to attend to, and dived into the nearest bank. It was to prove a move for which I thanked my lucky stars. A couple of days later, one sunny morning at about seven o'clock, I was in bed when I heard an unrelenting banging on the front door. Unhappily I had been less than tidy the previous evening, and a set of incriminating negatives was lying in the bedroom for anyone to see – including prying policemen whom I immediately realised were downstairs demanding entry.

The negatives were not alone in threatening to give the game away. Lying out of my line of vision behind the dressing-room door was a plate of the bright-green United States Treasury seal which graces the dollar. It was greatly enlarged, in order to assist my approach to some rather delicate artwork, and its presence would not have been easy to explain. I got out of bed with more alacrity than usual, wondering why on earth the police should want to see me, and locked the bedroom door to give myself a few extra moments in case they burst in. Then I grabbed the negatives in both hands while simultaneously searching for a hiding-place. I found one in the dressing-room, behind the fitted wardrobe. There was just enough of a gap between the back panel and the wall to which the wardrobe was screwed to slip the evidence. As I tipped the negatives down the gap I asked myself how the hell I should ever retrieve them when the panic was over, but that was the least of my worries as I bid them farewell. The sigh of relief which I breathed as they disappeared was premature; unfortunately I'd forgotten all about the Treasury seal.

By that stage the kids had let half a division of wild-looking policemen into the house (I can't remember where the wife was at the time) and they were banging on the bedroom door.

"Room service! We wanna see you, Charlie. So get your arse over to this door and open up."

"One moment. I'm just getting my trousers on. What's going on?"

My trousers only slightly above half-mast, I turned the key and had a search warrant thrust under my unshaven chin by an eager beaver of a police officer. I wouldn't swear that he was gloating but he did look particularly unpleasant at that hour of the morn. "What's this then?" two or three of them seemed to ask simultaneously as they gathered round the plate-maker. That discovery didn't much concern me because it was unrecognisable and passed as little more than junk. I mumbled a reply and they changed the subject to something altogether more sinister.

It transpired that the reason for their visit was an investigation into an armed robbery the other side of London. Now armed robbery has never been my kind of misdemeanour; perish the thought. So I must have looked genuinely shocked at the suggestion I had been involved in one. My difficulty was that some old fool who witnessed the robbery had identified me as a villain with a shooter from a rogues' gallery of mug shots shown him by the police.

I didn't know whether to be alarmed or angry. Do I look like an armed robber? Fortunately, however, it transpired that at the very moment the robbery was taking place yours truly was speaking to the cashier at the bank in Charing Cross. This rather attractive girl remembered me because I'd been stuck there for some time while some sort of discrepancy regarding the traveller's cheques was resolved. So the dear girl provided me with a perfectly proper alibi, bless her.

Her corroboration, however, could not help get me off the second hook by which I had been caught. The police never found the hidden negatives but they discovered the blown-up plate of the Treasury seal as soon as they walked into the dressing-room. Who could blame them for asking what I was doing with it? I was wheeled off to I forget which police-station in the City and deposited in a cell, next to which was a cage where was stored, like an accusing finger, the offending seal, plate-maker, chemicals and boxes of virgin plates.

It turned out to be fortunate that I had enlarged the seal from its natural size of perhaps half an inch to about eight inches. Its size gave me the fighting chance of protesting that if I were counterfeiting dollar bills then they'd have to be as large as a bloody football pitch. I explained, entirely in keeping with the truth, that I was a development engineer and that I was using the seal to experiment with the different values of ultra-violet and actinic light in order to make a prototype plate-maker. Actinic light, I explained, in as complicated a way as possible, in an attempt to blind them with science, were rays of short wavelengths which produce photochemical effects, whereas ultra-violet . . . I searched for signs of boredom or confusion on the faces of my interrogators. And I explained that all the paraphernalia they'd found at the house, were simply materials left behind by the police as immaterial to their prosecution of Stanley after the raid on Garden Road. Growing in confidence, I spoke of the relics of that period which, of course, had nothing to do with me as I was in prison.

Who was it said you can fool some of the people some of the time but not the whole police force every day of the week? While I managed to persuade the arresting-officer of my innocent intent I scored less well with his CID governor. Flimsy though I know some of the officers thought the case was, I was booked for counterfeiting.

It was a pretty serious matter and in moments of deep depression I despaired at the thought that my resumed career in counterfeiting was in tatters before it had begun. Fortunately, however, my barrister did me proud in court, pointing out that I must be a forger without camera, printing-machine or originals to counterfeit, if the prosecution case were true. I was actually convicted because I had technically committed an offence. But I got away with a conditional discharge and a fairly friendly warning from the judge. Moreover, all the equipment which had been seized was returned to me.

Sometimes I feel as if I have lived my life flying by the seat of my pants. As I retrieved my precious negatives from the gap behind the wardrobe, with the assistance of a large screwdriver and a larger supply of patience, I reflected that this was one of those occasions. A loss of memory by the pretty bank cashier would have banged me up for a crime I had not committed; equally, a moment's hesitation in disposing of the negatives would have thrown me from the frying-pan into the fire. The drama proved that once a villain's name is in the frame – as mine had been since I first went to prison – there it will remain, at the mercy of any policeman who fancies you for any misdemeanour.

It wasn't just from an early morning knock on the front door that I felt vulnerable. There was one occasion, I remember, when I was followed for miles by a police motor-cyclist – and it wasn't for bad driving. I was on my way to meet Brian – whom, incidentally, I never informed of my arrest for he would have run away from the partnership like a frightened rabbit. We had an arrangement to rendezvous in a café in Bognor Regis to discuss business. The police could not possibly have known that I was in the throes of setting up a counterfeiting operation and certainly, at the stage I was followed, Brian and I had not gone into production. But someone, somewhere, had taken a decision to make a target of me – a move which might last as little as one day or several months, or until the police find something better to do.

I was fed up with the route I normally took to Pagham or Bognor Regis so on this occasion I decided to drive straight to Brighton and turn right along the coast road. It was raining. Just outside Brighton I looked in my wing mirror and noticed several motor-cyclists behind me. They all overtook except this guy in a tell-tale white helmet, who held back one hundred yards or so. When I realised I'd seen the same rider on the M23 just outside London, the hairs began to rise on my neck.

I turned off the main road I was heading along and found myself on a housing estate. So did he. I stopped and got out of the car, clutching a map to ask a passer-by fictitious directions. The rider stopped too. When I moved off again so did he. At Arundel, near the castle, there was a roadside mobile café selling tea to truck drivers. I pulled off the road and bought a cup. My shadow also stopped and this time I could see him talking into a radio receiver. Brian was waiting ten miles away in Bognor Regis to talk through some problems he was having getting the ink right, and I knew that whatever I did, I must not lead my pursuer to my partner and a surprise pot of gold. I finished my tea, got into the car and performed a labyrinth of diversions until, quite suddenly, the rider wasn't there anymore.

I'm not paranoid, I assure you, but the events of that

afternoon forced me to stop the car a little bit further down the road to check there wasn't a helicopter on my side of the horizon. I don't know what my shadow's game was and I never shall. Maybe I was just picked as a pot-luck target. But I don't think it was that haphazard. I was two hours late meeting Brian in Bognor.

The two of us took no chances with security when we needed to make contact, as we frequently did. Brian would drive to a telephone box some way from his house and normally asked for George when he got through to my house. I'd reply that George had popped out and would be back in twenty minutes. That gave me twenty minutes to drive to a call-box where I rang him back at his (always supposing someone talkative hadn't dived in in the meantime), I didn't want to take the risk of using my own line when I knew there was a chance my phone had been tapped.

The code we used when we did confer on the telephone became more complex after we had gone into full dollar production and were printing to order. Dollar bills were usually "washers" – fifty-dollar bills were big washers and twenty-dollar bills small washers. How's this for an intriguing conversation?

"George? Hello."

"Hello, James. Everything OK?"

"Yeah. Just about to do a shift."

"Good."

"How many washers do you want?"

"Well big ones for a start."

"Fine. How many?"

"Well, do you know what?"

"What?"

"I haven't been feeling too well lately, to tell you the truth I haven't been feeling two grand."

"All right then, I'll have them for you on Wednesday."

"Usual place?"

"Yeah. Three o'clock."

The 2,000 fifty-dollar bills would be exchanged at a half-way point between Brian's house and mine – usually in the Dorking, Surrey, area at a pre-arranged car park. We'd park our cars side by side and maybe disappear for half an hour to talk business in a café. Then he'd open his boot and I'd open mine, each keeping an eye over the other's shoulder.

9

During the glorious twelve months in which my partner and I remained in unhindered production we must have forged dollar bills with a face value of over six million dollars – enough to satisfy the greediest of spenders in a capitalist society. Unfortunately we were caught red-handed by the counterfeit currency squad (which could scarcely have believed its luck) with half of this huge sum while awaiting a pay-off which would surely have made our fortunes. But, in the meantime, apart from one major incident, which seems hilarious now but which threatened to wreck our entire production, I would say Brian and I had a good working relationship. The contretemps between us involved a certain fellow by the name of Rover – an unpleasant brute of a boxer dog who took exception to the use of his bed as a hiding-place for a small quantity of dollar bills, which his master had arranged to purchase.

Thanks to the dog I found myself in the delicate position one day of having to explain to my exceedingly suspicious partner that the batch of fifty and twenty-dollar bills he had just printed to order had been eaten. "Oh yeah . . . and the rest," said Brian. You can imagine the performance which followed. He wouldn't speak to me for days. Worth the usual fourteen per cent of face value, the notes should have netted us about £1,000 each.

The dog belonged to a good friend of mine from Bermondsey, with whom I had previously done business, who wanted to buy the dollars for onward transmission to I know not whom. Although I normally insisted on cash upon delivery I agreed, on this occasion, to await payment a couple of days later. When I went round to his place to pick up the firm's £2,000 reward my mate didn't know where to put his face and even the dog looked a bit sheepish for once. The notes which he hadn't managed to swallow were in bits and pieces at the bottom of a cardboard box. My mate explained that he had hidden them under the dog's blanket for safe-keeping, reasoning that if the police should call he would order the vicious pooch to bed while the cops got on with searching the house.

Unfortunately Rover raked around his bed in the middle of the night, as dogs are wont to do, discovered the notes, and found them even tastier than a bowl of Pedigree Chum. Now I'm a reasonable man and, faced with the evidence of his midnight feast, decided there was no point in crying over spilled milk. But Brian was not a reasonable man and, just like our canine friend, howled for days, having convinced himself, no doubt, that he was the victim of a conspiracy between two men and a dog. Personally I believe that animals, like children, should be seen and not heard.

Curiously, in all important respects other than his income, Brian turned out to be a patient man, never once complaining, as something over eight months rolled by after the formation of our partnership, while I perfected the techniques involved in forging the perfect dollar. The greenbacks we eventually produced proved well worth the long hours of experimentation. Moreover, they defied even the most sophisticated equipment the United States Treasury was developing to keep the likes of me at bay. There were three innovations I was determined to implement before I allowed the presses to roll, and, for me, the most rewarding of these was the embossing of the dollar which gives it its special feel.

The offset litho process puts ink on the paper beautifully, but it leaves it as flat as a pancake, so I decided to try to raise the surface of the note to give it better authenticity.

I assiduously tried three methods to produce the desired effect. The first involved the purchase of half a dozen wire brushes which I ground down on a lathe so the hairs were of identical length. I mounted them on a spindle so they would revolve like a roller, but slowly, with the assistance of a low-power motor. The idea was to indent the paper in the imaged areas alone so it would feel as if the ink were raised, even though the resulting relief would not faithfully follow the contours of the filigree and fancy lettering. But the process damaged the paper, regardless of the care I took, and I was forced to abandon the idea after two wasted weeks of work.

Instead I turned to the application of thermography, a process of printing which involves the use of a heat source on the ink. After printing the dollar bill in the normal way, I sprinkled it lightly with white thermographic powder, which is resin based. Under heat, such as the wife's oven grill (a process best performed while she's not in the house), the resin combines with the ink so long as it's applied before the ink is thoroughly dry – normally within eight hours. The surface of the ink is thus raised rather as it is in posh letterheads.

After experimenting with a number of differently graded powders under Joan's grill, I thought I had cracked the problem of embossing the forgeries. But, of course, the grill did not allow for an efficient dollar production run any-more than the thermographic powder would have allowed my breakfast bacon and tomatoes to taste as they should. So I lashed out £350 on a purpose-built thermographic machine – a combination of conveyor belt and heated elements with a dish to take the powder. Brian, who was poorly paid in his employment as a jobbing printer, rarely had any spare cash, so it was nearly always down to me to pay for new equipment.

The powder, of course, fuses only with the imaged areas of the printed article and just dusts away from the rest. The speed with which the paper passes through the machine, and the degree of heat to be applied, are adjustable. Actually, true embossing requires the paper to be indented through pressure, but thermographic powder is cheaper and easier, and nowadays a well-acknowledged substitute. So, after choosing a matt, fine powder and acquiring the machine, which I took straight down to my partner, I felt we had the answer to a forger's prayer. I was wrong.

Brian telephoned me in no time to say we had a problem and ask me down for an inspection. The embossed notes he showed me when I arrived the next day were unbelievable. They looked like that short-lived phenomenon of late-fifties cinema, the 3-D film; the image leaped from the paper like a psychedelic experience. Brian explained he had used as little heat and powder as possible but the results were still way over the top. It was heartbreaking in a way, but I still had to laugh. Brian was doing nothing wrong and, try as I might, I could not improve on his performance. It was just that, unlike Joan's grill, the machine did too efficient a job for our purpose. So I had to abandon my costly investment and return to the drawing-board. I hate accepting defeat, especially when I know full well that I have hit upon the perfect technology for the job in hand but failed to master it.

I eventually solved the embossing problem by pressing the printed notes in a hand-press through thin cardboard, against a brass block into which I had engraved dozens of the most minute pyramid shapes with a V-cutter. These were so small they were imperceptible to the eye but your finger-tips were deceived into telling you the paper abounded with relief-work as if it were embossed. The pyramids were cut into the brass block to match the imaged areas of the note alone, so the paper felt smooth where it remained virgin.

The feel of a note is dreadfully important and although I would have preferred to have mastered a thermographic approach, I nevertheless ensured my forgeries passed the touch test. Embossing was the penultimate process in the production of the dollar bill, preceding only the glycerine-texturing finish. With its addition to the overall task of forging the greenback, from applying the lime-green tint to both sides of the virgin paper, to adding the red and blue fibres, to applying the black and green ink, to adding the Treasury seal and the various plate and serial numbers, to guillotining, to embossing, to glycerine-texturing, I am talking of a good dozen separate processes. Thoroughness and attention to detail have no substitute in my trade if the forger wishes to do his work properly.

Embossing, then, was the first of my three innovations during the partnership with Brian. It was a painful business though not half as painful as the second of them – well, it didn't hurt me actually so much as it did a Jewish solicitor who bought some of my forgeries second-hand. It was his unfortunate arrest in Geneva, very soon after the presses first began to roll at Pagham, which led me to realise that I was using the wrong paper. If he's reading this then I'd like to take the opportunity to apologise to him for the inconvenience I caused, and also to thank him. You see, his experience led me to switch to the Optimum 80 gram per square metre wove non-fluorescent paper which I have already mentioned in passing.

This is what happened. After beginning production in the summer of 1976 Brian and I turned out a sample run of about 30,000 dollars. Now it was my job to sell the notes, which I did to a contact who in turn sold some of them to the solicitor. Unfortunately the solicitor, a partner in a City firm, was not told, as he should have been, that the notes were counterfeit. Instead, he was given to understand they had been stolen. They looked so authentic – individually numbered out of sequence and, in appearance, like used notes owing to the glycerine-texturing – that he had no reason to disbelieve the story or feel he was taking a risk.

The poor man was keen on smuggling money into Israel though I don't know how he came to be in Geneva with my forgeries in order to execute his design. Anyway it was there he was arrested presenting the money to a bank cashier. Of course I wanted to find out what was wrong with it; no self-respecting retailer wants his customers incarcerated, because it's bad for trade. Eventually I discovered that the cashier ran the notes through an ultra-violet light box which exposed them as forgeries because they fluoresced, and promptly pressed the red alarm button.

So once again, having suspended operations at Pagham, I was forced back to the drawing-board to overcome a problem which I had not previously realised existed. I bought some ultra-violet lighting and started searching through a whole pile of swatches, which I borrowed from the principal paper-makers, for a paper which didn't glow. Finding one wasn't easy. In my experience only about three in a hundred do not fluoresce and, of these, many are for other reasons unsuitable for forging dollar notes.

I believe in learning the lessons in life so, once bitten twice shy, I did what the Swiss do and acquired a special light box – for use in my pet shop to ensure I never become the victim of a dud note. I keep it next to the cash register and pass every single note I'm handed through it to ensure it doesn't glow. It wouldn't do my reputation much good if someone slipped me a forgery, would it?

As a matter of fact my bank manager came into the shop one day only a couple of years ago to buy some seed for his budgie, or something like that, and when I ran his fiver under the light he raised an eyebrow and asked what on earth I was up to. He'd never seen such a device before, can you believe! Fortunately his surprise was greater than his sense of outrage that I might be implying he was the bearer of a bent note. I suspect only the bigger bank branches in this country possess such equipment. Curiously in the twelve years I have owned the shop, I have never yet been slipped a dud one though there was one genuine note which fluoresced because it had accidentally found its way into someone's washing machine. The absence of forgeries in my shop suggests either that there can't be many on the market or that pet owners are an unusually honourable collection of people. Unless of course it has something to do with my retirement from printing sterling.

My third innovation at this time was the application of magnetic ink, not just for the numbering of the notes but for the entire black filigree upon the front. Without anyone actually being caught for holding dollars without it, I got some early feedback from the States that some of the banks had started to use a security machine which "bipped" to confirm magnetic ink had been used. The easy availability of magnetic ink meant I had no difficulty in conforming to the standards of the United States Treasury.

Nobody but God and Brian knew what I was up to during my second venture into counterfeiting, though I daresay some people suspected it. I sold the notes through a handful of trusted criminal contacts but not even they were told I was actually forging. I just said I was acting for somebody else who was at it and how much he wanted for the goodies. There was no shortage of customers. I remember a particularly appreciative Spaniard, a hotel owner on the Costa Brava who bought dollars by the bucketful from one of my salesmen. It was a bit naughty but he was never told he was buying counterfeit currency; neither was his brother-in-law with whom he was working hand-in-hand. This man was a bank manager with a liking for dollar reserves in view of the weakness of the peseta. Whether the secrets of his beloved bank vaults were ever uncovered I do not know to this day.

I honestly do not wish to blow my own trumpet but I shall. Whenever, by chance, I had a mixture of genuine notes and forgeries in my possession – perhaps when I was abroad – I could not immediately tell which was which. Don't take my word for it. At my trial in 1979 Mr. Michael Coombe, who prosecuted me, sounded like a character from a television advertisement for Stork margarine. He made it plain to the Old Bailey that American Treasury experts had difficulty telling the difference too. But in the earlier batches I knew of one tell-tale sign under an eyeglass. In the middle of the bright-green Treasury seal on the front of the dollar note there is a pair of scales about a quarter of an inch wide. Imperceptible to the unaided eye, the merest speck was missing from the top right-hand corner of the balance which held the scales. How it came to be missing from the negative and plate I do not know but I'm certain no one else ever realised it. Diligence required that I restore it to its proper place for the subsequent series of forgeries.

Despite Treasury concern over the discovery of the unfortunate solicitor's fluorescent forgeries in Geneva, it was not until late 1976, several months after Brian and I got into full production, that the first non-fluorescent bill was spotted by officials. That was in New York and it set the cat among the pigeons, I'm told. Nevertheless all that was ever recovered, in the system, of the millions of dollars I put into circulation, was 8,200 dollars, despite the most intensive investigation – small beer when you consider that in twelve months my firm printed enough notes to darken the New York skyline like ticker-tape. For all I know some of it may still be washing around.

The only other city in which I know for sure my forgeries were discovered was Stockholm. These were from my first, fluorescent series. I had sent a package of them personally to Sweden in response to a cry for help from a friend on the run. They were concealed in the wrapping which I wound around a plastic egg – a perfect Easter gift except the season was wrong. I despatched the gift free of charge because that is the Christian thing to do for a friend in need.

The mate in question was the one doing porridge in Leyhill for killing his missus. Undaunted by this experience, the fellow had remarried, a beautiful Swedish girl in fact, almost as soon as he regained his liberty. The trouble was that he got a little too protective towards her one night when he returned home with a bellyful of beer and discovered a friend of his had escorted her home from somewhere else on his behalf without permission. Booze can do some dreadful damage to the brainbox and although my mate knew the fellow was a homosexual, with no designs upon his wife, he lost his temper badly and copped a charge of grievous bodily harm. So far, so bad. The next thing that happened was that my mate half-forgave his poofter friend and started seeing him again.

When your luck's down it tends to stay there. In no time my mate came under scrutiny from the police again. This time for allegedly interfering with witnesses. The poor man couldn't take anymore. With the threat of a long stretch inside again, he decided to leg it with his wife to Sweden. Unhappily the pair were boracic. Hence the sad appeal for funds which I received from him by letter one day. Could I place my hands on a little bit of surplus? Of course I could. I replied by return of post, telling him to expect a parcel within a week and advising him to eat or otherwise to destroy my letter. Now sending a bundle of forged currency through the post is not a wise course to take as a rule but the answer to the problem lay in a large yellow plastic egg which was filled with dried herbs. I don't know how it ever found a place in my house and I never liked it anyway, not least because of the smell it gave off. But my philosophy is never to throw out even the most useless object unless it bites you because you'll never know when it might come in handy.

I could not take the risk of stuffing the egg with forgeries, but I guessed the corrugated cardboard in which I chose to wrap it might do the trick instead. I cut pieces out of the packaging, laid a generous sum of dollars inside and spent a considerable time sticking other bits of cardboard on top. In the end I was left with some formidable criss-crossed packaging, not entirely in keeping with the worthless object it was supposed to protect, through which a Nosey Parker could see some daylight along the corrugations but not the secret cash. The whole operation was performed, of course, with the assistance of a pair of gloves. Then, with not a little pride, I posted the egg in the West End, without specifying the address of the sender.

I later learned that Swedish customs officers, or more precisely a pack of their sniffer dogs, took a fancy to the smell of it. So, no doubt believing they'd uncovered a cache of cannabis resin large enough for an all-night street party, the customs men ripped open the parcel with gusto. What should they not have done? Counted their chickens before they hatched. Oblivious to the content of the packaging, they must have puzzled over the peculiar things the English send each other abroad, resealed the egg, covered it with the original wrapping and allowed it on its way to my mate. When he opened it he thought it was no yoke either! "Charlie said it's here," he kept muttering to his wife, "but it isn't here." Only after reaching the conclusion that I'd made him the victim of a cruel prank did he have the nous to peel off the layers of wrapping.

I'm afraid the money didn't do him a lot of good. He spent a pile of it on new clothes for himself and his wife (I thought it was food he wanted) at a store prepared to accept American dollars. Only later was it discovered they were forgeries. But the astute shop-assistant who had served him spotted my mate in his new whistle in some remote part of the city and called for the assistance of a passing policeman. Whether it was the assistant or a bank cashier who discovered my pre-Optimum 80 glowed I really don't know.

Still, every egg has a silver lining. My mate served nine months on an idyllic prison island noted for its flora and fauna to which he was taken by aeroplane. So far as I'm aware he spent his time in the land of the midnight sun stuffing his face and making love to his beautiful Swedish wife. Working in the cookhouse, he helped himself to the best cuts of meat, while at weekends his missus joined him in the private bungalow specially allocated to prisoners to ease the passage of time in the best way nature intended. They say the French are the most romantic but I reckon the Swedes take the biscuit. Can you imagine the Home Office sending our Jack the Lads down to the Scilly Isles for unending sexual relief and three-course dinners?

Interestingly, however, my mate was also visited on one occasion by someone entirely less desirable than his wife. An officer from Scotland Yard's counterfeit currency squad arrived, bearing a short list of the names of forgers known to the police, to interview him. My moniker was somewhere near the top of it. But my mate was far too content with life to even think about dropping me in it. It was an irritating fact of life, which I was forced to accept, that I was always likely to be in the frame when the police went looking for the perpetrators of forged currency. Sometimes this could be quite offensive to me – notably when I observed the quality of some of the work put into circulation by my so-called rivals.

In February 1977, with the operation well oiled and production in full swing, came the break which promised to make me irrevocably rich. A heavy-duty, olive-skinned contact from Beirut, whose clients seemed to have their bejewelled fingers in every juicy international pie, approached me for some samples. When he liked what he saw and obtained the blessing of his masters he put their money on the table and ordered a cool two million dollars' worth of notes. I took the approach as a great compliment, cock-a-hoop that the reputation which preceded me should have attracted such international approbation. It represented a far cry from the days and nights when I was sweating to reproduce the Father Christmas photograph, though fewer than six years had actually passed by.

Brian, who had mastered the laborious printing techniques very well, and my good self had been making a comfortable living from regular orders here and there from a variety of customers whose blushes I shall spare (they were by no means all low-life characters, believe me). But the Beirut deal promised something different – an absolute killing. The long and the short of what followed was that I ended up one day driving down to Pagham with my jam-jar awash with virgin Optimum 80 to begin the task of printing enough money to make your eyes water. The boot, the rear seats and the rear floor were piled high enough with paper to make Edward Gibbon's *History of the Decline and Fall of the Roman Empire* shrink to the size of a pamphlet. As the miles whizzed by I could not stop myself, time and again, dwelling on the delightful equation:

$$\frac{14}{100} \times \frac{2,000,000}{1} = \text{ bloody rich}$$

The fourteen per cent of two million dollars which Brian and I stood to share (my arithmetic told me it was 280,000 dollars) would probably more than double the six-figure net income which we might have been approaching at the time the order was made. And then, who could tell, perhaps there would be a series of repeat deals big enough to leave standing the string of noughts which follows the biggest football pools payouts.

I should have learned the lesson of the egg and the Stockholm customs-officers – not to count the cannabis until it's hatched. A combination of two foolish mistakes conspired to wreck the whole counterfeiting operation. Only one of them was remotely down to me.

A very good friend of mine whose acquaintance I made in prison – a man with a penchant for stolen silver, which he bought at scrap value and resold at a somewhat higher rate – was friendly with a long-distance lorry driver. Although he had no financial need to involve himself in counterfeit currency, living a comfortable life in Somerset, he was always intrigued by my line of business and quite regularly bought pocket-money from me, usually no more than 1,000 or 2,000 dollars at a time, which he always paid for on the nail. I had just handed him a batch when I made

151

the Beirut connection, and he passed it on for a reason I know not to his friend, the lorry driver. Unfortunately this knight of the road chose to take the notes on a trip to Turkey in his waggon. Now if you've ever shivered at the treatment handed out to Brad Davis in his starring-role in the film *Midnight Express* you'll know that Turkey is not the most comfortable of countries in which to be taken prisoner; Turkish prisons make a cell in the Scrubs appear like a suite at the Ritz and the local jailors are likely to throw away the key once they've banged you up.

His pockets bulging with fifty-dollar bills, the silly fool of a lorry driver compounded the error of taking them there by splashing them around town as if they were going out of fashion. When he started lighting his cigars with them (I speak metaphorically) he not surprisingly attracted the attention of the sadists who masquerade as police there. Once he was in their custody he was unable to persuade them the money was legally his. The lesson he learned too late was that the last thing a criminal flush with cash – genuine or not – should do is draw attention to his affluence. Many a villain's euphoria over the acquisition of sudden wealth has betrayed him. The more he has, the less obtrusive he should be.

Threatened with the kind of discomfort one feels when strung up by the thumbs, the silly trucker decided discretion was the better part of valour; he coughed. More precisely he spluttered out the story of how he acquired the dollar notes as Turkish suspicion grew that they were not all they appeared to be. Thus our mutual acquaintance in leafy Somerset was unwittingly threatened with a spot of bother. The next step in the lorry driver's inquisition followed the arrival of a US Treasury official who flew in from Paris.

Apparently the Turkish police had to recover their American colleague's jaw from a level parallel to the floor, after he took his first look at the offending dollar bills. He was sure; he wasn't sure; he thought they might be; he called for better lighting; he called for a more powerful eyeglass. Chastened by the sight of such works of art, he accepted a drink before composing himself and sending for the lorry driver to whom he spoke in an interview-room. The terrified trucker was eventually offered a deal which was beyond his selflessness to refuse. The Treasury man told him that if he pointed the finger at his supplier he would be returned to England to stand trial; otherwise he would be left to rot in his Turkish cell without food or sanitation for the rest of his natural.

Half a continent away, two days later, something stirred in a delightful corner of the English countryside. A troop of English policemen invaded my friend, the silver dealer's premises. For once they weren't so much interested in the silverware which graced his home as the source of the dollar bills which he had handed over to the lorry driver. Searching for more counterfeit currency they went through the place like a dose of salts. Now my mate is a good'un and he would never have wittingly dropped me in it, so he never squealed. But unfortunately he'd made the daft mistake of recording my telephone number in pencil in the back of his passport. He might as well have added my photograph and written a caption with my name on. A police-officer, who was clearly destined for promotion, spotted the number. So there I was, smack in the middle of the frame as the counterfeiter. The next day the counterfeit currency squad arrived at Garden Road, mob-handed. To give him his due my mate rang me as soon as I got bail. Distraught over the sequence of events, he made profuse apologies and offered financial assistance. I declined but forgave him. He was a villain of the old school, with heartening supplies of humility and generosity.

Despite the arrival of the cops at my place I still believe I might have got away with it if it hadn't been for the conjunction of a second foolish error of judgment.

Since forming the partnership with Brian, I had made it a practice never to take anything home with me as incriminating as forged dollar bills. But the very night before the boys in blue burst in I broke my golden rule. That day I had supplied a customer – the last, I suppose, before concentrating on the Beirut contract – with a medium-sized order of greenbacks. As usual, according to my instructions, Brian had secreted them in the false bottom of a cardboard box and handed them to me in the aforementioned car park in Dorking. The trick was to obtain two grocery boxes from a supermarket, lay up to half an inch of dollars in the bottom of one, and then glue the close-fitting second box all the way round inside the first, taking care through careful cutting with a knife that the end product looked just like a single container. For the sake of authenticity we would finally pack a few vegetables in it, normally potatoes or, if the season were right, a few flower bulbs. It was a sensible precaution to take in case one of us ever had the misfortune to be stopped in a police trap or involved in an accident.

My customer had previously seen, through a middleman, some samples and approved them. After picking up the order from Brian my next move was to hand it over to the contact in Putney whose job it was to deliver it and take payment. When my man returned half an hour later to hand over the proceeds he still had the box containing the forgeries. Quite rightly he'd refused to release the goodies after the customer prevaricated and demanded a couple of days' worth of credit. We didn't know him well enough for my man to compromise the agreed procedure. So there I was, lumbered with a pile of forgeries.

I didn't want to take them back to Garden Road, but I had no real option. I could have taken them to my parents' house, I suppose, and asked them to look after them for me. But I didn't think it fair to put them at risk and didn't want to lie when they asked why I should be requesting the safe custody of a box of King Edwards! So I took the bloody things home with me and became the first man ever to be roasted by five pounds of potatoes.

Such is the luck of the draw that the single occasion I should take my work home with me should happen to coincide with a visit from the police. After being so careful throughout the time the partnership flourished, one slip and the whole venture blew out on me.

The cops banged on my door at the unusually civilised hour of ten o'clock next morning. I'd put the offending box overnight in the garage, reasoning that this is where most gentlemen store their spuds. A particularly shrewd policeman who picked it up decided it felt too heavy for the fairly thin layer of potatoes inside and executed a fatally comprehensive inspection. Most coppers would have just kicked it out of the way, so bully for him. It was just my luck, if you'll allow me to be a fatalist for a moment, to land the one policeman who would have made it to the rank of chief-superintendent in the weights and measures department at the town hall. That was it; goodbye Charles Black.

Although they found only these forgeries and no counterfeiting equipment at Garden Road, the search-party summonsed the cavalry and so I finished up with a whole battalion from the counterfeit currency squad pouring over the place like a crowd of hungry shoppers at the January sales. In the loft they found a Mauser pistol – missed over the years by previous police search-parties – and a quantity of ammunition. I hasten to add I'd never used it nor intended to. Why did I keep it? Just fascination for the thing I suppose, and no more threatening than relics brought home from the Second World War by large numbers of tommies. There was also a gas gun, similarly unused. In addition the police found a counterfeit gold five-pound piece whose origins I cannot remember and a forged half-sovereign. This wasn't by any standards a bad haul for three days of searching though I knew nothing much about it at the time because I'd been banged up in a cell at Bromley Police Station.

Before I forget – they also found 5,000 pounds' worth of

which they were convinced were forged but which were not. When they returned them two years later to Garden Road the value of the peseta had plunged from about 110 to the pound to about 170, if my memory serves me correctly, though maybe a currency speculator, such as myself, had no right to complain.

There was one piece of evidence the police uncovered in my house which was to prove of far greater value to them in cracking the organisation and putting Brian out of business than the rest put together. It was the frame number of my partner's printing-press which I had written down on a scrap of paper more than a year earlier to enable me to order parts for it. Another astute detective recognised it for what it was and, through tracing the manufacturer and supplier, was able to lift the unsuspecting Brian in Pagham. He immediately put his hands up because that was the only sensible thing to do. It would have required the combined talents of a magician and a politician to deny the existence of a forger's den at the back of his garage. No doubt he believed that I shopped him, but that was the least of my worries. After appearing on remand with him on a number of occasions and finally in the dock at the Old Bailey I have never seen him since.

Under interrogation I resolutely denied counterfeiting any currency myself, but could scarcely deny the presence of a bundle of forged greenbacks on my premises. Things did not go entirely against me in the wake of the raid however. I contrived to strike a deal with the police which gave me my liberty on bail during the eighteen months in which I awaited trial. The cops were naturally anxious to trace all the negatives and plates, knowing that without them there was a risk the operation might be resurrected by others elsewhere. Now it so happened I had only given Brian the plates from my negatives, not the negatives themselves. The police threatened and cajoled when I nodded them the wink of their existence but I refused to reveal where they were unless they guaranteed not to oppose bail. When they said they'd find them anyway without my assistance I shook my head confidently, knowing they never would. In the end the police were forced to do a deal and keep me out of custody. The negatives were once again stashed inside the hollowed-out portion of the kitchen door.

It was because I put up the barricades and refused to admit conspiracy to forge, that the case took eighteen months coming to court. My stubbornness forced the police to spend a very long time looking for witnesses, gathering evidence and assembling a case. If I had just put up my hands their job would have been a thousand times lighter and I'd have been in the dock as quick as a flash – all teed up nice and easy for the judge to send me away. The truth is I intended all along to change my plea to guilty once I got to court, which I did. I put to good effect the eighteen months of liberty, but it was little compensation for the feeling of disbelief that at the point of cleaning up, I had been cleaned out.

The case was heard at the Old Bailey on January 5, 1979, but in the intervening period I managed to amass enough money to pay off a £10,000 mortgage, buy a new car and purchase the pet shop which I have to this day.

Some of the money came from consultancy work I supplied to a well-known professional footballer who had decided that, well paid though he was, there was insufficient reward in the game to provide for his retirement and the lifestyle to which he was accustomed. I suspect he is as aggressive off the pitch as he was on it, so I shan't take the risk of naming him. Anyway, I set up for him a hydraulic press to forge half-sovereigns – employment, you will remember, of which I had previous experience – and all the necessary gold-plating machinery. The introduction was made by a man who already possessed the dies for stamping the coins. There were a few notorious "faces" who were involved with the footballer in putting up the capital. In a somewhat delicate position owing to my impending appearance in court, I merely showed them what to do and then stayed well out of sight while the half-sovereigns popped out like coins from a fruit-machine. They were stamped out of copper, dipped in gold and then inserted in gentlemen's rings. I seem to remember that when the operation was busted, several months after my association with it, the police also found some two-pound dies, though I'd never seen them during my brief involvement, and that these were to form the basis of a further counterfeiting venture.

At my trial, as I listened to Michael Coombe prosecuting, I could not help but feel his remarks sounded more like an oration in honour of my skills than an indictment. He told Judge Mervyn Griffith-Jones that the one-and-a-half-million-pound face value of the dollars seized at Pagham was the fruit of just about the biggest counterfeiting and distribution ring ever organised in Britain. His Lordship positively seemed to sit on the edge of his throne as Mr. Coombe, who is himself now a judge, pointed out the notes were almost perfect and that the naked eye could not detect them as forgeries. When the judge later asked to examine some samples his Lordship made a point of remarking how authentic they not only looked, but felt.

"Thanks to the Optimum 80, the embossing and the glycerine-texturing," I said to myself. "He might be about to bang you up, Charlie, but at least he has the grace to recognise true craftsmanship when he sees it."

The judge was not the only one to be impressed. A United States Treasury expert regarded them as the best that had ever been produced, the court was told. I glowed with not a little pride.

But I wasn't altogether pleased with what Coombe went on to say, and gave my ex-partner, who was sitting beside me in the dock, a less than brotherly glance. The prosecutor explained, from what Brian had told the police, that I – a "stranger" – had recruited him at a printing exhibition with the seductive offer of easy cash and had "used" the poor man. No comment will suffice. Like me, Brian pleaded guilty to conspiracy to forge. For good luck I also put up my hands to the other charges of which I alone was indicted: counterfeiting the gold five-pound piece and half-sovereign, and possessing the pistol and ammunition, gas gun and cartridges.

The point I found most interesting during the trial was Coombe's revelation that the United States Treasury had spent millions of dollars perfecting a machine to detect counterfeit currency – but that the forgeries I had produced were so good they made it obsolete. That was the most telling measure of the expertise I had acquired in the eight years since entering the field of play. Quite what the machine was I'm uncertain, though I imagine it combined magnetic ink security recognition with testing the inert qualities of the paper. It seemed such a dreadful shame that I should be at the point of enforced retirement when the highest Criminal Court in the land had witnessed a public admission that I was one step ahead of the United States Treasury. By no means did I vow to myself that the Treasury had heard the last of Charles Black, master forger, when I left the dock.

Mind you, I had something other than the Treasury and its damned machine on my mind as I descended the steps to the cells below the Central Criminal Court. Namely, my sentence. Brian got three years, which seemed reasonable to me. But, expecting something similar, I got ten, and that was not the end of it. Judge Griffith-Jones went on to reel off a whole series of terms for the minor misdemeanours as if he were reciting the London telephone directory. My sentences added up to twenty-one years, leaving me feeling as if I had won a game of pontoon and been forced to pay off all the other players. Fortunately these annoying little additions to the sentence were ordered to be served concurrently, so I actually ended up with a debt to society which promised to keep me out of circulation until 1989. The ten years for conspiracy was, I believe, the heaviest sentence ever handed in this country to a contemporary currency counterfeiter, and it was doubtlessly aimed at cutting off my fingers while they still possessed such skills. I appealed against sentence and was rewarded with a three-year reduction to seven years. In fact I emerged from Maidstone Prison in the spring of 1982, having served only three years and four months, for which I offer my deepest thanks to the Parole Board.

At the time I was put away I had failed to make real money out of counterfeiting – you know, the kind of big money which would inspire a Labour government to send the taxman after me with a whip. Counterfeiting is one way of becoming a millionaire and that was the driving force behind me, the carrot before my nose as I put millions of dollars into circulation during my partnership with Brian. The fact that I did not furnish the financial system with enough forgeries to make a fortune means, in a sense, that I failed. But for me there was, in another sense, a rich reward; the achievement of forgeries as close to perfection as is humanly possible in an exciting exercise which bucked the system. I was, according to some of the friendlier coppers I got to know, a walking danger of unprecedented degree to the banking system. I should add, however, that though I made enough money to pay for some of the finer comforts in life (exactly how much I cannot be sure) it was insufficient to compensate for the amount of time I served in prison.

After nearly a year in Wandsworth I was transferred to Maidstone where I followed previous experience and knuckled under immediately. Sure enough, in no time at all I was allocated to the prison print-shop where I suppose I was regarded as something of a celebrity. The governor, who was a perfectly nice fellow, took me along and said with a grin: "Right then, Black, let's see what you know about printing?" I like a good sense of humour. I re-organized the shop for him and was invaluable when it came to repairing any of the equipment which went wrong. In fact more than one screw at Maidstone had to hide a tear when I finally bade them farewell. My status, and the fact that my family was only an hour's drive down the road meant that my incarceration was relatively tolerable. But who wants to be locked up year after year? Not me.

I came to the conclusion there was no way for me to operate safely in this country while mine was the counterfeit currency squad's favourite mug shot. But abroad? That's different. The only way to operate with cast-iron security is with the sponsorship of untouchables like Colonel Gadafi in Libya, Fidel Castro of Cuba or perhaps the Mafia. Don't imagine this is just a fanciful idea. There are people and organisations who might find it in their interest to establish and protect a top-quality forger. Consider why: a state-sponsored dollar counterfeit racket in countries where the United States is considered the *bête noire* of the universe would provide not just weapons for "freedom fighters" around the world, but undermine the American economy. What a weapon unlimited billions of dollars would be in the hands of Gadafi and his fellow travellers! And huge secret criminal societies like the Mafia who sometimes have law enforcement organisations in their pockets? Well, they would never say no to the profit and power currency counterfeiting brings. I have no doubt such possibilities have occurred to the United States Treasury.

Personally, I've never received an invitation from Tripoli and have stuck to my decision never to counterfeit again without foolproof protection in a foreign country. In Britain there are too many hurdles to keep jumping, once you are known to the police. There are some who make it and some who don't. I count myself as someone who nearly made it.

Meanwhile, let me say that the determination of the judge to render me impotent was not entirely successful. While I was in Maidstone I received a visit from a friend. Our conversation was not one which would have been approved by the prison authorities, whose often liberal policy on admitting visitors sometimes surprises me. My friend explained he was calling on behalf of a forger who specialised in printing building society cheques, but wanted to expand. Most stores accept such cheques so this forger, who was unknown to me, had taken advantage of the situation by buying expensive watches and fur coats for his wife. But he'd run out of things to buy, as one does.

None of the merchandise was much good for easy, profitable re-sale. Thus his decision to print money. My visitor asked on his behalf what advice I might be able to supply and, after I'd outlined it, the forger came to see me. For £1,000, which was duly paid into my account, I was able to provide him with a lot of useful information about photography, printing, paper, ink, numbering boxes – in fact as much of my expertise as could be furnished in a one-hour visit. I envied the forger his opportunity but I could not afford to be envious when my consultancy fee in prison for sixty minutes' work was possibly five times as much as the governor earned in a week.

As well as counterfeiting consultant I became a teacher of the subject in Maidstone. For six months before my release I taught an underworld heavy in the print-shop how to counterfeit currency, so that, by the time he too left prison, he was as proficient in the theory and much of the practice as necessary to build his own forger's den with the backing of others. But the man, Nicky Gerard, was shot dead at the age of thirty-two soon after his release in an underworld revenge killing for the death two years earlier of another criminal, Alfredo "Italian Tony" Zomparelli. Ten years before that I had been the man responsible for getting Zomparelli out of the country when he was on the run from the police for yet another killing. Although I detest violence I was thus indirectly involved in three killings.

The story started in 1970 with a telephone call at home one day from Fred. The big man knew that I had a lot of friends and contacts in Ramsgate on the Kent coast. Some of them owned boats and this, he thought, might be of assistance in getting Italian Tony, an acquaintance, out of the country and the long arm of the law. Fred said the man was so hot that he needed to be found a safe house in the London suburbs for a few hours. He was not just on the run from the police, you see, but half the underworld who wanted to get him for stabbing to death a brother of Ronnie Knight, then the husband of *Carry On* film actress Barbara Windsor, in a nightclub brawl.

This is how I came to harbour Zomparelli for the best part of a day while I was on the blower to a few close friends in Ramsgate. Eventually I got hold of a friend with a motor cruiser, whom I'd previously met in prison where he was serving time for smuggling tobacco from Holland. For a hundred pounds my mate agreed to take Italian Tony quickly to France. He was a sound bloke so Fred, who was desperate to get things moving, agreed immediately and arranged Zomparelli's transfer to Ramsgate. To cut a long story short Operation Overlord swung into action and our hot property was dropped off on a beach in Normandy, where he was picked up by previous arrangement, and secreted by contacts somewhere in France.

Quite how long he was in France I'm not sure, but after some time, Fred informed me, a deal was struck whereby Zomparelli put his hands up and returned home to face not a murder charge, but manslaughter. I think he got about four years. But in 1980 the underworld caught up with him, as it normally does in the end. Italian Tony was shot dead in an amusement arcade.

This is where my counterfeiting protégé Nicky Gerard comes into the picture. Gerard, a nightclub bouncer, with a baby face, who was said to be heavily involved in protection rackets, was charged with Zomparelli's murder, together with his friend Ronnie Knight. But both men were acquitted in November, 1980. Gerard had been paroled only six months earlier from a seven-year sentence for the shooting of East-ender Michael Gluckstead.

How did I come to meet him? Well by coincidence,

with only six months of my sentence left to serve, I was approached by some heavy duty people at Maidstone – armed robbers and the like. I was not naturally part of their circle and did not seek to be but, because of the respect accorded a forger in prison, I was on good nodding terms with them. For some time I had felt they regarded me as someone who might some time in the future be of use to them. They would get their money by taking a shooter into a bank instead of a cheque-book; I would get mine by more peaceful means. So I think I intrigued them.

Anyway, one day I was asked by them if I would do them a great favour, and it seemed to me sensible not to refuse. They told me they had a mate who had just been transferred to Maidstone to finish off the last six months of his sentence for I'm not sure which particular piece of villainy. The man in question was none other than Nicky Gerard, and the job in hand was to teach him how to become a forger. A violent man like him would not normally have been my ideal choice of pupil but he seemed respectful enough to me and I agreed to try to get him a job in the print-shop as a machine-operator.

This I had little difficulty in arranging. A trusted prisoner who took the work seriously while others just messed about, I had the ear of the screws who were grateful for my expertise. With a little pushing and shoving it was thus agreed that Gerard could join me. Moreover he was allowed to start work immediately on an offset litho whereas most newcomers were given the most menial tasks, like folding paper.

Now Gerard had no previous experience of printing but he did have a very sharp mind and took to the subject like a duck to water. Furthermore his motivation was positively voracious. I talked to him hour after hour, day after day. But of course I omitted to mention that I was the man who'd helped the geezer Gerard was acquitted of murdering to escape. Loose talk kills. And it wasn't my fault that such a coincidence existed, was it?

For six months I taught Gerard everything I knew. Some of it, such as the camera work, the colour separation and artwork, was inevitably only in theory because this side of the forger's equipment is not readily available in prison. But the handling of printing machinery and plate-making was a different matter. In the finish he picked my brain clean as a whistle. I took him over everything, step by step by step. In Maidstone all we had was time. Gerard had a few thousand pounds put by for a rainy day and he was so taken by the idea of investing it to print more that he shone as my pupil. He wanted me to go over everything time after time until, in the end, I was like a walking text book, even in my sleep. But I didn't mind. I loved the subject anyway, and it was fascinating to discover how it took a hold of him too. In the end we even grew quite fond of each other and, between relating hair-raising stories of his violent life on the outside, he suggested how we might be able to get together after we'd been released. Gerard finished up an accomplished printer in offset litho, flat-bed and platen machinery. In fact, when he emerged from Maidstone in 1982 at about the same time as I did, he knew considerably more about the art of counterfeiting than I had when I was trying to teach myself ten years earlier.

Unfortunately he went out and got shot in the head almost as soon as he got released, and never put my teaching into practice. It was such a waste. Gerard, a much feared man as a gangland enforcer, was killed on June 25, 1982. The poor man, I gather, had been in a real party mood the day of his death – his daughter's eleventh birthday. He'd just given her a perfumed love-heart as a present, sung Happy Birthday, kissed his wife and popped down the road for a drink. But he never reached the pub. Two men wearing boiler suits and balaclavas got in the way just after he left his house in Stratford, East London. They gunned him down as he sat in his car. With blood pouring from his chest he jumped out and ran fifty yards.

It was to no avail. His executioners fired two more shots from their sawn-off twelve-bore shotguns, the newspapers said. Both missed but they caught up with him and clubbed him to the ground. As he screamed for help one of them reloaded and shot him through the head. He was a good family man; it's strange how so many villains are.

Before and after I had finished paying my debt to society, I received two interesting job offers. Both were abroad; both meant improved security of the kind I have previously said was of paramount importance before I would even think of going into production again. The first was in Lisbon. The offer was to work under cover at a bona fide printing factory which also specialised in turning out bogus trading stamps. What was required of me was to develop a new line of merchandise: forged dollars. But I never got the chance of inspecting the premises, which I suspected were not secure enough anyway. So I turned the offer down.

The second was to work for an Australian, a man at the top of the police "Wanted" list in his own country who was temporarily residing on the Costa Brava. I went to see him after an introduction had been effected by a well-known member of the criminal fraternity. After meeting him in South London and talking business the pair of us flew to Spain.

There I met his Australian acquaintance who turned out to be none other than Robert Trimbole – the notorious drug smuggler who bribed politicians and police-chiefs, and threatened school children when they refused to harvest his marijuana crop. Trimbole died of a heart attack in Spain in May, 1987 at the age of fifty-six, and the world is better off without him. He was the man who wrested control of the "Mr. Asia" syndicate after a series of murders. The syndicate had for years flooded Britain and Australia with huge quantities of heroin.

Trimbole came from Griffiths, a small town on the edge of the desert in New South Wales which grew rich on his criminality. Many of its inhabitants were Italian immigrants from Plati, a stronghold of the Calabrian Mafia who supplied Trimbole with cash to plant a marijuana crop there. He recruited schoolchildren at four pounds an hour for the night-time harvest of the crop.

The man fled Australia in 1981 after being tipped off by corrupt policemen of his impending arrest, and took with him the register of deaths in Griffiths from which he took out passports in the names of the deceased. After first fleeing to Ireland he moved on to the Costa Brava. There I met him in a sumptuous apartment where all his needs were taken care of by his beautiful mistress and a large drinks cabinet. He turned out to be an incongruously charming little man with a pot-belly and a beach hat, as well as a back pocket stuffed with the biggest roll of hundred-dollar bills I had seen since going to prison. What did he want of me? He had a plan to set me up in an advanced forger's den of my own design backed by a large expense account. Trimbole offered to provide premises in their own grounds in Spain or in Italy. But after two fairly lengthy conferences, conducted in the most relaxed manner, I turned him down. Whatever he suggested I was forced to conclude that security would not be a hundred per cent perfect, even though it would be better than anything I was likely to find in Britain. It also occurred to me that I didn't fancy being anyone's employee.

I have always wondered why it is that people who claim to have developed the perfect system for winning the football pools should want to advertise a service to the public offering "guaranteed" winnings. If the mastermind behind the scheme is so damned good why doesn't he bank a million pounds every week of the season and keep damned quiet about how he does it. I felt a little like a man with a proven system being asked to win the pools for someone else. Why should I?

When I came out of prison in 1982 it was to find Britain dominated by a woman in 10 Downing Street, and my own life dominated by another little lady at twenty-eight Garden Road. Long-suffering Joan, my companion of twenty-five years, decided she'd had enough of me. She tackled me like the Prime Minister was tackling the trade-unions and announced she was putting an end to my influence on marital matters by divorcing me. I suppose we'd grown apart anyway after such a long time, much of it spent in enforced separation. She wasn't so much miffed by my regular withdrawals from circulation as by the regular supply of police-officers at the front door. Who can blame her when their search-warrants not only entitled them to turn me over but poke about amongst her own innocent belongings?

Joan was not all that pleased either when, as soon as I came out of Maidstone, I set off for Malaysia and Thailand to follow up suggestions I had received for the perfect site to set up another forger's den. The visit to Thailand, though I was not to know it at the time, was to alter my whole approach to life.

10

During my final year as a guest of Her Majesty at Maidstone I became a Moslem. No, it was nothing to do with a roll of thunder, a blinding flash of light and the religious conversion of Charles Black Esquire, lapsed Roman Catholic. But in a strong sense it had much to do with my quest for a new Mecca. My conversion was an expedient to enable closer association in prison with a Malaysian Moslem commonly known to screws and inmates alike as Sid. The pair of us wanted to indulge in intimate conversation about counterfeiting currency, a mutual interest, but the opportunity for long, private discourse under normal circumstances at Maidstone was limited. Sid, a likeable lad in his mid-thirties who was serving a long stretch for smuggling drugs into Britain, worked in the prison library where silence was golden.

In snatched conversations Sid told me he had been involved in forging Malaysian money many years before, but its quality was so poor it had to be dumped in the Strait of Malacca or some such waterway. Meeting me revived his interest in the subject while, for my part, the association opened up the possibility of establishing a new den on the other side of the world, where I was rather less well-known. There was no question of my printing Malaysian currency, whatever that is, if I were to take such a step but I could think of no reason why I should not return to dollar production there if the circumstances proved right. But how were my new friend and I to get down to detailed discussions?

Sid overcame the problem one day when – just as

Mohammed must have exhorted his followers – the lad said: "Why don't you come down the mosque?" This Mohammedan place of worship was actually a single room in the nick which had been kitted up with an altar and other bits and pieces. Moreover, it was screw-free. Just a few guys with impressive looking dreadlocks, whom I suspect regarded Islam as the fashionable faith to follow, plus a handful of Arabs, most of whom seemed to be in prison on account of their criminal misuse of kitchen knives, drifted in and out of the mosque. What the place would mean to Sid and me was several hours of almost uninterrupted conversation every Friday – so long as I could persuade the prison governor to accept my religious conversion and change all my records.

Now the governor of Maidstone in those days was a bit of a Bible basher who may not have had as high an opinion of the Koran. So I spent at least a month trying to convince him of my honourable intentions, ignoring the sniggers of screws and inmates along the way. But in the end he agreed.

Thus it was I eventually found myself an incipient follower of Mohammed, my accoutrements consisting of a prayer mat, a string of ivory beads and a skull cap – all gifts from Sid. Interrupted only when I took instruction on Islam and Allah from an imam, I spent many unholy hours plotting secular improvement with my Moslem friend. There was however one heavy price to pay. It was called Ramadan – the daily fast from dawn until nightfall which is rigidly enjoined during the ninth month of the Moslem year. Now a rumbling belly seems to me particularly unhealthy, especially in a man of sixteen stones, so I forced myself to scoff the occasional snack when no one was looking during my spiritual journey.

If I felt a bit conspicuous in my faith at first, I'm not prepared to say. But Allah works in strange ways. The curious thing is I became quite interested in the faith and have remained a Moslem ever since, albeit of the non-practising variety. It seems to me that if a man should take a faith he should take it seriously.

Sid, a man with a wealthy background who only took to importing drugs in order to finance his insatiable appetite for the casinos of Kuala Lumpur and the European capitals, provided me with invaluable information on the idiosyncrasies of counterfeiting in South-East Asia. After we were released from Maidstone we corresponded, and then one day he telephoned me at the pet shop to arrange a counterfeiter's fact-finding mission to Malaysia. I agreed to fly out to see him but explained there might be a delay on account of a shortage of cash. The next thing I knew, a first-class air ticket arrived in the post at Garden Road from which he must have got little change from £3,000.

During my two week sojourn in the delightful city of Johor Bahru on the South Malay Peninsula, where I was provided with Sid's permanent private suite of rooms at a five-star hotel, I talked at length to him and his associates about the ways and means of adding a new dimension to the economic life of Malaysia. But it turned out to be a very small country in all senses of the word and a place likely to be fraught with difficulties for a forger, not least one used to the by-ways of England. I felt from the inquiries I made that I'd probably be able to obtain all the right equipment for a den and, certainly, there was no shortage of financial backing. Moreover I suspected the forces of law would be less vigilant there than in England, given Sid's excellent connections. But I could not be certain of overcoming all the problems I expected to face in such a monumentally different environment. And I did not want to make promises to potential associates which I could not keep. What if the ink dried too quickly or the air conditioning affected it and the huge range of other materials, I wondered amongst many other things. The conditions were simply not right, not least because it was so bloody hot outside I felt as if I'd been smacked in the face with a steaming-wet towel.

Undeterred by my reluctance to go into business in Malaysia, Sid suggested we fly to Thailand where he also had a network of wheeler-dealer connections who might be helpful to a forger looking for premises. Thailand sounded to me a bit more exciting than a wet week in Brighton so, I thought . . . in for a penny, in for a pound. I kept an open-mind but my reservations about starting a den anywhere in South East Asia were growing by the day. Sid, of course, detected my hesitance but our firm friendship was not affected, and anyway he enjoyed introducing me, as a westerner, to his influential acquaintances.

We landed in Bangkok and I have left my heart in that exquisite land of smiles ever since. The time is not far away now when I shall sell up in England and retire there. It was that first visit to Thailand in 1983 which changed my life. You see, I fell in love with Thai women. I don't mean the beautiful creatures who populate the liberated massage parlours of the Phatphong Road, though they put a spring in the step of the most jaded traveller, it is true. I mean the multitudes of pretty girls to be found in every street and on every narrow waterway. What is more, these enticing, graceful creatures have remarkably good taste for they appear to adore the company of Englishmen, especially as their own men, whom they far outnumber, often treat them with a complacency which I find shameful. I had no doubt that lonely Englishmen at home would feel as warmly about Thai girls as I did – if only I could get them together.

And that is how I came to set up my marriage agency. I realised I no longer wanted to be a counterfeiter. The lonely hearts business was for me. Finding beautiful Thai women who wanted to marry Englishmen was easy – they wanted to come to England to be properly cherished in a more liberated environment in which their prospects and those of their children were better than at home. The problem was sending my first Englishman to Thailand and getting him home safe and sound with his lovely bride. No one really knew what immigration or other difficulties might put a spoke in the wheel of true love. So on the advice of a solicitor I decided the only course was to send a guinea-pig. And who should be the subject of the experiment? It had to be me, of course.

Freshly divorced as I was, I did not relish spending the rest of my natural as a lonely man and, with time's winged chariot flashing by, concluded the moment had arrived to remarry. I wasn't short of encouragement if I had any doubts about the venture. Members of my family were constantly telling me to tie the knot again. With my international mating agency at stake the enterprise seemed an ideal way of killing two birds with one stone.

Upon arrival in Bangkok in August 1985 I was prepared, by previous arrangement, to meet over seventy girls during the following few days – a heavy task, I don't think. In the end about twenty expressed a desire to marry me. I've never felt so wanted in my life. Two days into my visit a heavenly creature called Deer walked into the office I had set up with the help of a Thai associate. She was twenty-six and she ran a hairdressing business with her sister. We were married three days later in a registry office and during the few days which followed my lovely bride obtained, with the help of a lawyer, a Thai passport in the name of Mrs. Black, and a visa from the British Embassy consular section in Bangkok. Thus I got what I had set out to get – a beautiful wife and the practical experience of acquiring all the papers necessary for a Thai bride to accompany her English husband to England. When Charles Black makes up his mind nothing stands in his way.

You might think all this sounds extremely unromantic. Not a bit of it. It's not in my nature to be boorish. Deer and I spent a week's honeymoon among the palm trees at Pattaya on Thailand's Riviera about one hundred and fifty kilometers south-east of Bangkok where we enjoyed the tropical ambience and each other, the way newly-weds normally do. She spoke little English and I little Thai so we just talked the language of love.

Deer and I weren't in love immediately, I suppose, but deeper love followed a few months later as we formed our lives together. She was a little homesick for a few weeks, missing the bustle of Bangkok, but she has come to love England and, anyway, both of us return regularly to her paradise on the other side of the world where we plan to settle. We have two beautiful sons, Mark, born on December 21, 1986, who is bilingual now he has stopped gurgling, and Simon, born on April 30, 1988. The dear lady finds me handsome, which I am of course, and the thirty years' difference in our ages matters not a jot. I could not have made a better choice of wife.

Deer's arrival at Heathrow brought not just a glow to my heart but my pocket too. I knew I was in business as a marriage broker. Having proved it possible to bring a Thai bride to England without legal difficulty, I advertised the agency in London listings magazines and waited for the response. A number of clients came along and the first three flew to Thailand in January, 1986. All returned home with their brides without complication. In the past two years I have played Cupid to over thirty clients and, at the time of writing, there are as many again waiting to fly to Thailand, where as many as 450 girls want to meet them with a view to marriage.

Deer and I have now set up home in Chislehurst, Kent, in a house where nappies and playpens are rather more common than photographic plates and ink. As a matter of fact I'm still waiting for a Blue Plaque to be fixed to the wall beside the front door of my old house in Garden Road. It would say "Charles Black, Master Counterfeiter, lived here". And I'd be pretty proud of it even though those industrious years brought their share of grief as well as elation.

Now I'm well established in the lonely hearts business

174

– and earning a good living from the pet shop – I have no need to earn money by printing it myself. In any case it was a dire shortage of the stuff, as well as the challenge of counterfeiting, which led me up that dizzy path in the first place. Moreover, with my sixtieth birthday behind me, I'm in the mood for retirement.

I have gone straight but that's not to say I don't experience the odd hankering to beat the Bank of England. The smell of ink never leaves the nostrils; ask any printer. I know my expertise is going to waste but I tell myself that when a man possesses skills too dangerous to use he's better off ignoring them. You might be the best knife thrower in the circus but you sleep better at night if you're one of the clowns. All I can say is that I gave counterfeiting my best throw when I had the motivation – and stabbed myself once or twice in the process. What's more, I sleep at night now knowing the police aren't going to be opening my garden gate before the milkman gets there. From bitter experience I know I should hate to waste another day of my life in prison no matter how liberal the régime there might be.

Of course I keep abreast of developments in the currency business, in an academic sort of way you understand. But I can't say that since I've retired from it I've seen many significant new challenges for the forger. Somewhere or other I've read that the greenback is going to be printed in unforgeable paper. Such a suggestion tends to make me smile. I always think that if a man with a machine can devise a new security system – whether it be in currency or inter-galactic defence – then another man with another machine will devise a means to overcome it. I should think something like a hologram of the kind which features on cheque and credit cards would have to be introduced to a bank-note before I were to feel seriously challenged. But I'm quite sure if I put my mind to it the hologram could be overcome. It's only a trick of the light, after all, like the watermark. Since paper has been used as currency it has been forged and I've no doubt it always will be, regardless of its sophistication. Just think of a combination lock. If you can work out the sequence then you can open the safe. You just have to be intelligent enough to anticipate what has been built in to a system to defeat you.

I mean, look at the weaving of the silver strip in the ten-pound note nowadays. What would that require of a competent forger such as myself but simply to print a broken line in silver ink? In-between, where the line does not show except under light, I should revert to the familiar practice of drawing a line in black ink before applying opaque.

In fact many of these so-called security defences make the forger's job easier. People will look for that special distinguishing mark to check it is there and scarcely examine the rest of the note. I have a feeling that if a forger substituted Napoleon for the Iron Duke on the back of the fiver then, so long as the watermark was there, the average punter wouldn't take a blind bit of notice.

Now retired, perhaps unwillingly, from the field of forgery, CHARLES BLACK today makes an honest living as the proprietor of a Thai bride agency.